BREWSTER & CO
NEW YORK

Dietrich Inc.
DETROIT.

FLEETWOOD

HOLBROOK
HUDSON, N.Y.

JUDKINS

Le Baron

WILLOUGHBY

THE COACHBUILT PACKARD

A beautifully restored 1940 Darrin Convertible Victoria, owned by the Pettit Collection of Louisa, Virginia. The original catalogue in Mr. Pettit's possession says, "Here is a car to make heads turn and hearts sound . . ."

THE COACHBUILT

HUGO PFAU

DALTON WATSON LTD
LONDON

First Published 1973

ISBN 0901564 109
Library of Congress Catalog Card Number 73-77557
Copyright 1973 in all countries of the
International Copyright Union by Dalton Watson Ltd.

All rights reserved

Process Engravings by Star Illustration Works Ltd.

Printed in England by the Lavenham Press Ltd.
for the publishers
DALTON WATSON LTD.
76 Wardour Street, London W1V 4AN

Distributed in the U.S.A. by
MOTORBOOKS INTERNATIONAL
3501 Hennepin Avenue South
Minneapolis
Minnesota 55408

Preface

When the idea of this book was first broached, I had in my files somewhat over one hundred photographs or other illustrations of Coachbuilt Packards. Many of these were pages from old magazines or other sources which could not easily be well reproduced.

Unlike the situation in Europe, where many coachbuilders files had been preserved, most of the American firms had gone out of business prior to World War II and the material they had accumulated during their careers was often destroyed. For instance, I was told some years ago that the photograph files of LeBaron, including hundreds of pictures I had shipped to Detroit when we closed our New York office in 1930, had been discarded because space was needed for other purposes. Only after I had made this statement in print did I learn that a very few, perhaps a dozen or two, such photographs had been preserved by a later employee of LeBaron and I was able to have these copied. They included a couple of Packards which appear herein, and I am grateful that Ted Pietsch had the foresight to save at least these few.

A limited number of photographs from the files of other coachbuilders did find their way into various collections, and I was able to obtain a number of Willoughby and Derham pictures from Henry Austin Clark, Jnr.'s Long Island Automobile Museum, and also some from the Seaman Body Company through Mr. John Conde of the American Motors Corporation, of which Seaman was one of the predecessors.

Fortunately, I was aware that the files of the Detroit Public Library had recently been augmented by a large collection of photographs from the old Packard files, which had been donated to them by the successor to the Studebaker-Packard Corporation. Having already delved into these to a limited extent, I knew that they were not catalogued or properly sorted. Many of the pictures were not even fully identified.

With the assistance of James J. Bradley, head of the Automotive History Collection of the Detroit Public Library, and of my friend Jack Triplett, who had also done some browsing among those pictures in research for The Packard Club, I had at least some idea which of the many boxes contained pictures of custom bodied cars. It still took many hours to segregate these. For some, negatives were available, but others had to be rephotographed, a job excellently done by Joseph Klima, Jnr. About one-third of the pictures herein are from this source.

Most of the pictures in this collection were of cars with bodies that had been ordered in series by Packard—anywhere from five to twenty-five or more of one design. There was a sprinkling of individually styled bodies, but only a fraction of the ones I knew had been built.

Several years ago, John F. Dobben, former chief engineer of the John B. Judkins Company, had sent me copies of some articles written by his son, and illustrated with photographs of various Judkins bodies. Unfortunately, his son had died suddenly shortly after the articles were published, and in the aftermath the original photographs somehow disappeared. Some of the Judkins illustrations are reproduced from their previous publication and may not be of quite the quality we have tried to maintain.

Other pictures I have obtained from the present owners of coachbuilt cars or from contemporary magazines in which they had been pictured when new.

To Hermann C. Brunn and Enos Derham—each of whom headed his family's custom body business for a time—and to John F. Dobben of Judkins, Rudy Creteur of The Rollston Company, Raymond H. Dietrich, Ralph S. Roberts and R. L. Stickney, with all of whom I worked at LeBaron, and to Thomas L. Hibbard—to all of these thanks—for many hours of pleasant reminiscing which recalled bits of history.

To Jim Edwards of Harrah's Automobile Collection, Don Butler, William S. Jackson, Lord Montagu of Beaulieu, William A. C. Pettit III, Shelley D. Vincent, Raymond M. Wood, and the many others who contributed photographs or information, thanks also.

H.P.

Acknowledgment

The author and publishers would like to record their sincere appreciation to the following persons and organisations for supplying photographs and drawings illustrated within and for their permission to reproduce them.

Automotive History Collection, Detroit Public Library, pages 14, 15, 17, 19, 22, 25, 26, 29, 31, 32, 33, 34 top, 35 lower, 36, 37, 38 top, 40 top and bottom, 41, 43, 44, 45, 46, 48, 49, 50, 51, 52, 53, 54, 55, 56, 57, 58, 59 top, 62, 64, 65, 68, 69 lower, 70 lower, 71 centre, 73, 74 lower, 75 top, 78, 79, 80, 81, 82 top, 83 top, 84, 85 centre, 86 top and bottom, 87 top and centre, 88 top, 89, 90, 91, 92, 93, 94 lower, 95 top, 96, 98 lower, 99, 100 centre, 103 top, 104 centre, 110 top and centre, 112, 113 lower, 116 lower, 118, 121 centre, 122, 123, 124, 128 lower, 129 top and centre, 130, 131, 132 lower, 135 top, 140 lower, 144 lower, 145 top, 146 top, 147, 148, 149, 150, 151 lower, 152 top and centre, 156 top, 158, 161 centre, 164 lower, 165 lower, 166, 167 centre and bottom, 168 lower, 169 lower, 178 top, 179 lower, 186, 187, 188 top, 192 top, 193, 194, 195, 196 centre and bottom, 197, 205 top, 206 lower, 212, 218 centre, 222; Automobile Manufacturers Association, Detroit, Mich., pages 114 top, 115 top and centre, 117, 120, 145 lower, 155 bottom, 213; American Motors Corporation, Detroit, Mich., pages 200, 201, 202; Henry Ford Museum, Dearborn, Mich., page 269 top; Harrah's Automobile Collection, Reno, Nev., pages 39 lower, 95 lower, 97, 216 lower, 217; Long Island Auto Museum, Southampton, N.Y., pages 59 lower, 71 bottom, 72 top, 74 top, 75 lower, 88 lower, 111, 113 top, 114 centre, 156 lower, 171 bottom, 173 lower, 182, 183, 184, 204 top, 216 top; Museum of Automobiles, Arkansas, page 198; National Motor Museum, Beaulieu, England, pages 172 top, 189, 204 centre, 214, 221 lower, 223; Gustaf Nordbergs Vagnfabrik, Stockholm, Sweden, pages 218 bottom, 219 top and centre; Mr. Donald Butler, Detroit, Mich., pages 104 top, 160 top, 180; Mr. John F. Dobben, Newmarket, N.H., pages 134, 135 centre and bottom, 136, 137, 138; Mr. Andrew Henderson, Grosse Pointe, Mich., page 106; Mr. Phil Hill, Santa Monica, Cal., pages 108, 109, 191; Mr. William S. Jackson, Hummelstown, Pa., pages 30, 39 top, 42, 63, 82 lower, 100 top, 129 bottom, 190, 210, 211 lower; Mr. Jerry W. Jones, Indianapolis, Ind., page 104 bottom; Mr. Lars Kile, Jr., Christianssand, Norway, pages 34 bottom, 38 lower, 101 top, 105 top, 173 top,

207, 211 top, 218 top, 219 bottom, 220, 221 top, 224; The Pettit Collection, Louisa, Va., pages 3, 171 centre; Mr. Robert A. Phillips, Wichita, Kan., pages 102 lower, 170 lower, 172 lower; Mr. Ted Pietsch, San Diego, Cal., pages 154, 157; Mr. Richard Quinn, Mokena, Ill., pages 35 top, 98 top, 161 bottom, 188 bottom; Dr. Larry Quirk, Tucson, Ariz., page 176; Mr. Fred Roe, Holliston, Mass., page 144 top; Mr. Ralph Snyder, Mount Joy, Pa., page 178 lower; Mr.Mark Sternheimer, Richmond, Va., page 159 lower; Mr. Shelley D. Vincent, Mendon, Mass., pages 72 lower, 102 top, 170 top; Mr. Raymond M. Wood, St. Albans, Vt., pages 94 top, 100 bottom, 103 lower, 105 lower, 121 bottom, 128 top, 192 lower.; Mr Paul Womersley, Bradford, England, page 206 top.

Contents

CHAPTER ONE

The Packard Chassis

Early Packards

James Ward Packard and his brother William were already successful manufacturers of arc-lights and other electrical equipment in Warren, Ohio, when they became interested in automobiles. They bought several cars in Europe during the 1890s, then came one from Alexander Winton, the Cleveland automobile pioneer. After driving this for a time, they made some suggestions to Mr. Winton, prompting his comment that if they thought they could build a better car, they should do so.

The Packard brothers accepted the challenge, formed a partnership with two Winton employees, George L. Weiss and W. A. Hatcher, under the name of Packard & Weiss, and before the end of 1899 had produced their first car. It was a single-cylinder affair looking somewhat like the buggies of its day.

The next year, the name of the company was changed to Ohio Automobile Company, although the cars were called Packards. In 1901, one of their cars was purchased by Henry B. Joy, a young Detroiter of considerable inherited wealth. He liked the car so much that he not only invested in the company, but persuaded some of his friends to do so as well. By 1903, the company was moved to Detroit, and its name changed again to Packard Motor Car Company, as which it was to continue for over half a century.

James W. Packard continued as President of the company, but his brother remained in Warren running their electrical business. Actually, it was Henry Joy who was the guiding genius behind the early growth of the company. By 1909, its capitalization had been increased to $10,000,000, and the following year Joy hired Alvan Macaulay away from the Burroughs Adding Machine Company to become Packard's General Manager.

In 1916, Macaulay became President of the company, a title which he retained until 1939 when he assumed the less demanding post of Chairman of the Board of Directors. It was during Mr. Macaulay's reign that Packard achieved its greatest prestige and its most profitable years.

Although the first Packards were small vehicles with one cylinder engines, they soon followed the pattern of other automobile manufacturers by growing both in size and in complexity. Under Henry Joy's prodding, a four-cylinder model was introduced in 1903, and by 1907 this had developed into the Model 30, which was a good sized car capable of carrying limousine bodywork on its longest wheelbase. By 1911 a still longer chassis was available.

Although coachbuilt limousine and landaulette models were available from the Packard factory, this chassis attracted the attention of prosperous customers who had it fitted with custom bodies from their favourite coachbuilders. To a more limited extent, this was also true of the smaller Model 18.

In 1911, Packard introduced its first six-cylinder model, and the following year expanded this to two sizes, Models 38 and 48. These model numbers were based on the S.A.E. horsepower ratings, which followed the same formula used in Britain by the R.A.C. and which was widely used for tax purposes. American licence fees were lower than abroad, which accounts in large part for the relatively larger engines used there.

Model 30 (illustrated opposite page)
Brief Specifications 4 cylinder side-valve engine.

Bore	5 inches
Stroke	$5\frac{1}{2}$ inches
Capacity	432 cubic inches
Wheelbase	121 inches in 1907
	123 inches from 1908
	129 inch long wheelbase added in 1911
	Short wheelbase runabout chassis,
	108 inches 1907/11
	114 inches 1911/12

Model 18 was similar in general design, but smaller.
Brief Specifications 4 cylinder side-valve engine.

Bore	$4\frac{1}{16}$ inches
Stroke	$5\frac{1}{8}$ inches
Capacity	263 cubic inches
Wheelbase	112 inches
	Runabout chassis 108 inches

Model 48 (illustrated below)
Brief Specifications 6 cylinder side-valve engine.

Bore	$4\frac{1}{2}$ inches
Stroke	$5\frac{1}{2}$ inches
Capacity	525 cubic inches
Wheelbase	138 inches in 1912
	143 inches from 1913

Model 38 was similar in general design but smaller.
Brief Specifications 6 cylinder side-valve engine.

Bore	4 inches
Stroke	$5\frac{1}{4}$ inches
Capacity	414 cubic inches
Wheelbase	134 or 138 inches in 1912
	140 inches from 1913
	Runabout chassis of 115 inches
	in 1912/14.

The Packard Twin Six

The outbreak of war in Europe in 1914 brought substantial experimentation with multi-cylinder engines to power aeroplanes. Interest in this development spread to the United States, where Cadillac introduced its V-type eight in 1914.

By the following year, Packard had capped this with its new Twin-six, a V-type twelve cylinder model which continued as one of America's most prestigious cars for almost a decade. Its design was supervised by Colonel Jesse G. Vincent, who had earlier worked for Alvan Macaulay at Burroughs. It was one of the most powerful engines put into any American passenger car up to that time.

Col. Vincent was also involved in the design of the Liberty engine, another "Twin-six," which powered many Allied planes during the latter part of the first World War. Packard was one of the leading suppliers of this engine and its production kept them quite busy although they still managed to turn out some automobiles during the war years. The lessons learned in mass producing aeroplane engines were to be invaluable later.

Although shorter and lighter than its six-cylinder predecessors, and initially somewhat less expensive, the new Twin-six had such smoothness that it soon became a favourite among coachbuilders and their clients both in America and abroad. It was the first Packard model to be fitted with a really significant number of custom-built bodies. By 1917, Packard was able to issue a catalogue illustrating more than twenty different designs from four of America's leading coachbuilders, which could be ordered through any Packard dealer at set prices.

At the New York Automobile Salon in the autumn of 1921, twelve different Twin-sixes were shown on the stands of five of the top coachbuilders in the country. It might be well to explain that the Automobile Salon, originally a showplace for the leading European imports, would not permit American manufacturers to exhibit their cars under their own aegis. The American chassis were admitted only as exhibits by the leading custom body builders, who were permitted to show their handiwork.

While the general size and the basic engine of the Twin Six remained the same throughout its life, up to the last few produced in 1924, there were many detail improvements from time to time. More noticeably, and inspired in large part by the fresh designs of the coachbuilders, there was a striking improvement in appearance. The later cars were much sleeker and smoother than their predecessors.

Along with this new car, Packard introduced a new system of model designations which was to continue through 1931. The first digit represented the series — which might last anywhere from a few months to several years — and the last two digits corresponded to the last two of the wheelbase. The first Twin Sixes of 1915 were called Models 125 and 135, which was also their wheelbase. Sometimes during the following year, these were changed to Models 225 and 235, and then during 1917 to 325 and 335. The latter numbers were retained to the end of Twin Six production, even though this was the period of greatest stylistic improvement.

Twin Six
Brief Specifications   12 cylinder, V-type, side-valve engine.

Bore	3 inches
Stroke	5 inches
Capacity	424 cubic inches
Wheelbase	125 and 135 inches, 1915/1917
	128 and 136 inches, 1917/1919
	136 inches from 1920

The Packard Single Six

When it was first introduced as a less expensive companion to the Twin Six, the Single Six was a much smaller car of only 116 inch wheelbase. Not many special bodies were mounted on it, but some did find their way on to the later 133 inch long wheelbase model.

With the introduction of the Eight in 1923, which had many inter-changeable internal parts, Packard also inaugurated a new policy. Chassis of the two cars were almost identical from the bonnet back, so that the same bodies would fit either Six or Eight. As a result, many of the custom bodies ordered in small series for the Eight would also fit the Six. Quite a few were mounted on the latter, especially for the export market where the smaller engine carried a much lower tax and had other operating econo-mies. For the same reason, a number of six-cylinder chassis were exported to be fitted with special bodies by leading British and European coach-builders.

This policy continued from the Models 126 and 133 — again rep-resenting the wheelbase — of 1922, through Models 526 and 533 of 1928, although changes in engine size and other refinements were made during this period.

Single Six
Brief Specifications 6 cylinder, in line, side-valve engine.
Bore 3⅜ inches, enlarged to
3½ inches in 1925
Stroke 5 inches
Capacity 268 cubic inches, enlarged to
288 cubic inches in 1925
Wheelbase 116 inches, 1920/1922
126 and 133 inches, 1922/1928

The Packard Eight

After World War I, costs kept rising and the Twin Six was becoming rather expensive to manufacture. Packard sought to develop a simpler design which would lend itself to the mass production techniques they had learned, but give the smooth performance associated with the Twin Six. After experimenting with various types of engines, they found the answer in an eight-in-line with a very rigid 9-bearing crankshaft.

At first there was some question what they would call this new model. Catalogues were even issued, identical except for their covers, calling it the Single Eight, the Straight Eight, and simply the Packard Eight. The latter was finally adopted after studying public reaction.

This designation was retained for half a dozen years, so long as it was the only eight-cylinder Packard. When a similar but smaller eight-cylinder engine replaced the Single Six for the 1929 model year, the larger car was called the Custom Eight or the DeLuxe Eight, depending on its wheelbase. Then in 1932 it became the Super Eight and this name was retained through to the end of production just after the entry of the United States into World War II.

There were some changes in engines during this period. The early ones had the same bore and stroke as the six, so that many parts would be interchangeable. Along with the Six, the bore was enlarged during 1926, and in this form the engine continued to power Packard's largest Eights until the autumn of 1936. The 1937 models introduced at that time used the smaller engine of what had been the Standard Eight, and then for the 1940 models begun during late 1939, a new engine was designed somewhat between the other two in size, and continued until 1942.

The in-line engines were longer than the V-twelves, and required a longer bonnet as well as a longer wheelbase. Both these developments appealed to designers, and inspired a host of new ideas from coachbuilders on both sides of the Atlantic. The timing was also good since the middle and late 'twenties were a period of great activity among American custom body builders.

During most of its life, the Packard Eight was made in several chassis lengths, and naturally most coachbuilt bodies were placed on the longest. There were some exceptions, notably in two-seater sport models, for which Packard at times made a special short-wheelbase version.

For the first few years, the long wheelbase was 143 inches, and bodies built for this could be mounted almost without change on the 133 inch long wheelbase Six. With the introduction of the new small eight in 1928, the large one was first produced in 140 inch wheelbase, with bodies interchangeable with the long wheelbase of the small eight. Soon a longer, 145 inch wheelbase chassis was also produced to serve as a base for custom bodies and lengthened versions of some standard models. These were no longer interchangeable with the small eight, something that will be discussed further in connection with that model.

Also, a partly experimental car was produced by mounting the large eight cylinder engine in the shortest chassis frame available, with 126 inch wheelbase, and called the Speedster Eight. Open sport bodies, modified from those in regular production, were fitted to the few of these cars produced. The following year, the Speedster Eight was continued, but now with the 134½ inch wheelbase of the longer small eight but retaining the large engine. More body styles were offered.

The Dietrich convertible bodies were redesigned to fit the 140 inch wheelbase of the large Eight, which again made them available on the smaller Standard Eight in its long-wheelbase version. However, most coachbuilders preferred the 145 inch wheelbase, which was continued as Model 745-C. Some people objected to the availability of only the most expensive coachbuilt bodies on this long chassis, and so Packard offered another choice, Model 745. This carried the same bodies as Model 740, including the Dietrich convertibles, but had its engine set somewhat further back and the hood made five inches longer, so that the space from cowl to rear was identical with Model 740. It was somewhat more expensive than the latter, but it had some of the prestige of the coachbuilt models offered on this wheelbase, at lower cost than those.

This multiple arrangement was discontinued with the end of the model year, and for 1931 the Model 840 chassis carried not only Dietrich convertibles but also a new series of town car and limousine bodies with Packard Custom Body Division nameplates. These were also available on the long wheelbase of the Standard Eight, Model 833. Outside coachbuilders still preferred the longer Model 845 and fitted their bodies to this.

With the beginning of the 9th Series, late in 1931 as a 1932 model, the longest wheelbase became 147½ inches. Now this was the chassis for all custom bodies, including those from Dietrich and Packard. This practice continued for the next few years, with bodies interchangeable between the large Eight and the new revival of the Twelve.

At the same time, the numbering system was changed again, with the two lengths of the large, DeLuxe Eight becoming 903 and 904. A similar system was continued, with the first digit representing the series, and the last two a sort of code indicating the wheelbase. Even the last of the prewar Super Eights had such official designations, although they were more generally known as the 160 and 180.

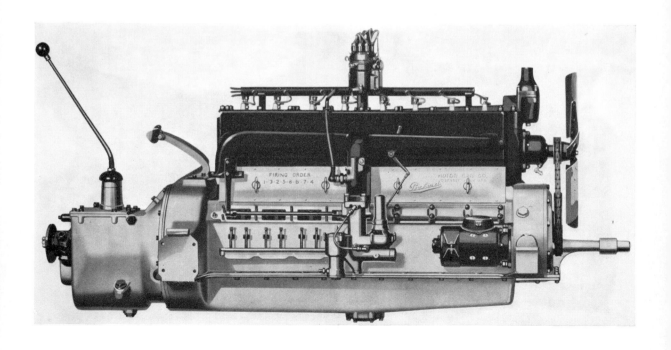

The Packard Eight

Brief Specifications 8 cylinder, in line, side-valve engine.

Bore	$3\frac{3}{8}$ inches, enlarged to
	$3\frac{1}{2}$ inches in 1926, reduced to
	$3\frac{3}{16}$ inches in 1936, redesigned to
	$3\frac{1}{2}$ inches in 1939
Stroke	5 inches until redesigned to
	$4\frac{5}{8}$ inches in 1939
Capacity	358 cubic inches in 1923/1925
	385 cubic inches in 1926/1936
	291 cubic inches in 1937/1939
	356 cubic inches in 1940/1942
Wheelbase	143 and 136 inches, 1923/1927
	143 inches, 1928
	126 inch Speedster, 1929
	$134\frac{1}{2}$ inch Speedster, 1930
	145 and 140 inches, 1929/1931
	$147\frac{1}{2}$ and $142\frac{1}{2}$ inches, 1932
	142 and 135 inches, 1933
	147, 142 and 135 inches, 1934
	144, 139 and 132 inches, 1935/1937
	139, 134 and 127 inches, 1938
	148 and 127 inches, 1939/1942
	138 inches also, 1940/1941

The Packard Standard Eight

For the 1929 model year, Packard replaced its Six with a smaller eight-in-line, called the Standard Eight. Like its predecessor, it came in two wheelbase lengths, the longer of which would accommodate the same bodies as what was now the shorter chassis of the large Eight.

Dietrich convertible bodies would fit both types, and a few were sold on the smaller chassis. However, other American coachbuilders were designing their bodies for the longer chassis of the large Eight, and these were not interchangeable.

Since there was some demand in other countries for town cars on the smaller chassis, a few custom bodies were ordered for it by Packard's Export Department. These were individually designed and built, and often more expensive than similar ones purchased in small series for the large Eight.

By 1931, not only were the Dietrich bodies available on the small Eight, but Packard had arranged to have some town car and limousine bodies built under its own name, which were also interchangeable. Things changed again the next year, but by 1934, for the Twelfth series, some town cars were again being offered, of identical design, on both large and small Eights.

Then, in 1936, the Packard branch in New York ordered some town car bodies on the still smaller Model 120 which in essence had replaced the small Eight. The following year, Darrin built his first experimental bodies, also on the Model 120. Similarly, a few coachbuilders in Britain and on the Continent offered some of their wares on this smaller chassis.

Standard Eight
Brief Specifications

8 cylinder, in line, side-valve engine.

Bore	$3\frac{3}{16}$ inches
Stroke	5 inches
Capacity	291 cubic inches
Wheelbase	133 or 126 inches in 1929
	$134\frac{1}{2}$ or $127\frac{1}{2}$ inches in 1930/1931
	$136\frac{1}{2}$ or $129\frac{1}{2}$ inches in 1932/1933
	141, 136 or 129 inches in 1934
	139, 134 or 127 inches in 1935/1936

Although the Model 120 was introduced in 1935, it was not until a somewhat larger version replaced the original one, for 1936, that it was fitted with coachbuilt bodies to any extent:

Brief Specifications   8 cylinder, in line, side-valve engine.

Bore $3\frac{1}{4}$ inches
Stroke $4\frac{1}{2}$ inches
Capacity   282 cubic inches
Wheelbase   120 inches in 1935/1937
            138 inch long wheelbase in 1936/7
            127 inches from 1938 on
            139 and 148 inch long wheelbase
               in 1938/1939

The Packard Twelve

For 1932, Packard again answered the challenge of multi-cylindered competition by reintroducing a V-twelve, and in fact for the first year bringing back the old "Twin Six" name. The new engine was even larger and more powerful than the earlier V-12, and one of the smoothest running powerplants on the market.

During the next few years, it served as the base for most of the coach-built Packards, until it was discontinued at the end of the 1939 model year. The chassis was designed so that bodies were generally interchangeable with the Super Eight, but many customers who wanted a more distinguished car elected to pay the extra cost of the Twelve, which varied from a few hundred to over a thousand dollars.

As with the Super Eight, most coachbuilt bodies were mounted on the longest wheelbase available, although a few open sport models were fitted on a special short chassis made just for them.

The Packard Twelve

Brief Specifications	12 cylinder, V-type, side-valve engine.
Bore	$3\frac{7}{16}$ inches
Stroke	4 inches
Capacity	473 cubic inches
Wheelbase	147 and 142 inches, 1932/1934
	135 inch short chassis, 1934
	144 and 139 inches, 1935/1937
	139 and 134 inches, 1938/1939

CHAPTER TWO

The Packard Custom Body Division

From the days of the first Twin Six, Packard took a direct hand in the purchasing of custom coachbuilt bodies, and for a time even offered some carrying a bodybuilder's plate identifying them as products of the "Packard Custom Body Division."

The Packard distributor in New York throughout this period was actually a subsidiary of the parent company in Detroit, operating under the name of The Packard Motor Car Company of New York, and some of the early custom body catalogues were prepared and issued by this branch. One of the New York executives, Grover Cleveland Parvis, was placed in charge of such activities in 1919 and continued in the post for a decade and a half. He placed orders not only for individual bodies for specific customers, but for small series of various types, with leading American coachbuilders.

By 1925, Packard's sales in this field had grown considerably and a Custom Body Division was set up in Detroit in charge of Horace W. Potter. For the next couple of years he handled the purchase of bodies in small series — from ten to as many as a hundred of one design. Mr. Parvis still ordered individual bodies for some customers who wanted something more unusual.

When it became apparent that many of the leading coachbuilders, largely concentrated in the East, preferred to deal with Mr. Parvis, purchases from them in series were again made by him. The Detroit people, however, handled the business with Dietrich who was located in that city.

Towards the end of 1928, Packard hired away from LeBaron, Raymond B. Birge, who had been managing their Bridgeport plant and had impressed Packard by the improvement in quality which he had achieved. In 1930, it was announced that he would be in charge of building a new line of custom bodies "by Packard."

Actually, Packard had no facilities for this work, but they leased a portion of the Murray plant. This company owned Dietrich, Inc., and was also building the Packard standard bodies at the same time. The new "Packard Custom" bodies were town cars and limousines, and were first offered on the Series 840 chassis in the autumn of 1930. Like the Dietrich bodies at the time, they were also available on the Series 833 chassis of the smaller Eight. The following year, somewhat larger bodies of the same general type, plus a few additional styles, were offered on the longest wheelbase of the large Eight and the new Twelve.

Soon this experiment palled and Packard resumed purchasing coachbuilt bodies from outside firms. A few of those carrying their own nameplate were still unsold and were offered on the Tenth Series chassis.

At the same time, Edward Macaulay, son of Packard's president, became actively involved in Packard styling. He came up with some rather radical ideas, a few of which were built for his personal use or as show cars. Since Packard did not have suitable craftsmen for such special work, these were actually built by the LeBaron-Detroit Company, but carried the nameplate of the "Packard Custom Body Division" rather than that of the actual builder.

One other activity for which this name was used was the building of bodies for the Speedster Eights of 1929 and 1930. The standard Packard bodies would not fit these special chassis, but were modified by the Murray Corporation, using a substantial portion of the front, at least.

The department was continued right up to World War II, but henceforth purchased the custom bodies offered in the Packard catalogues from outside coachbuilders. It was directed by Wellington Everett Miller, who had had previous experience with several custom body firms.

In addition to these activities by the Packard company, there were also some dealers who were especially interested in coachbuilt bodies for their own markets. Alvan T. Fuller, later Governor of Massachusetts, was for many years the Packard distributor in Boston. He ordered bodies from Judkins especially, since they were nearby, for his own use and for wealthy customers.

Philadelphia was another good market for coachbuilt Packards, and the distributor there worked closely with Derham to create special town cars and other types for his most discriminating customers.

Earl C. Anthony was the Packard distributor in California for most of the company's existence. In the early days he maintained a small body shop of his own, and later worked closely with such coachbuilders in the area as Murphy, Larkins, and Bohman & Schwartz. Some of these went to well-known movie stars in his clientele.

Finally, the Packard Motors Export Corporation, which shared part of the facilities of the New York branch, would often order individual bodies for shipment abroad, often quite different from those available in the United States. Also, their various distributors in other countries would import a certain number of bare chassis to be fitted with coachwork by local concerns.

The Packard files identify this only as a 1908 Model 30 "Special Limousine" without indicating the body builder. The rear section is very similar to Packard's own Limousines. A leather canopy over the windscreen helped to protect it from rain.

A 1907 Model 30 Touring Car with fixed roof and windscreen. Note rolled-up side-curtains strapped to the roof.

Another Packard body was this Limousine, also on a 1907 Model 30 chassis. The windscreen and front section of the roof are almost identical to those on the Touring Car.

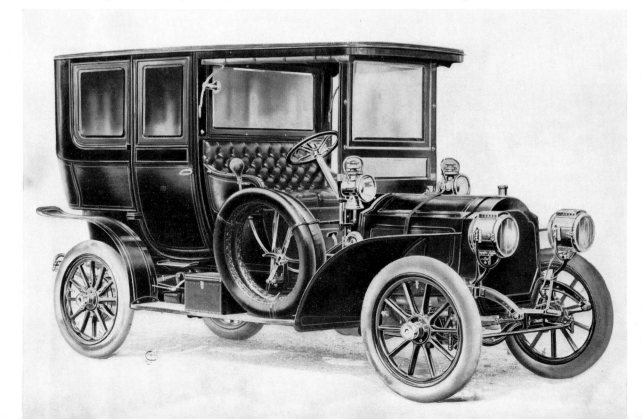

The Packard stand at the 1910 New York Auto Show featured this "Imperial Limousine" on Model 30, from their own shop.

A Model 30 Landau from 1911, with rear section of roof opened.

This Model 48 Town Brougham of 1913/14 seems to have been modified from Packard's standard Limousine, with a different superstructure.

Nathan Lazarnick, premier automotive
photographer of the time, took this picture in
1913 here reproduced in three parts but
failed to record the source of the bodies.

The Phaeton could be from Holbrook,
but the two closed bodies appear to be
Packard's own.

A Packard-built Limousine-Landaulet on a 1913/14 Model 48. Packard advertised their bodies as "interchangeable" and offered them for sale separately, this type at $1,850. One was urged to buy a tourer for $4,950 plus an extra closed body for winter use, with the total cost little more than that of one closed car, but with double the utility.

An early Twin-six Roadster, from 1915, at a Packard Club meet.

This 1916 Twin-six Tourer was fitted with special equipment for use by the Finnish Army.

Opera singer Anna Held with her "Milk White Limousine" on a 1916 Twin-six. The colour scheme of white and cream was reputedly inspired by her famous milk baths.

Catalogue drawing of a similar Model 2-35 Twin-six Limousine, which sold for $4,715 in 1916.

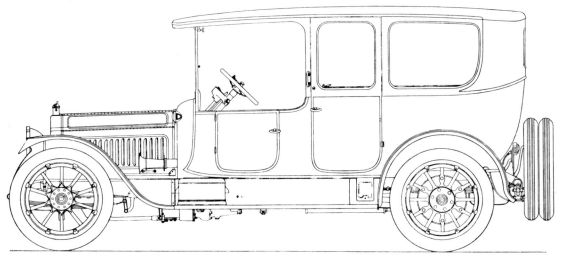

A 1916 Limousine-Landaulet by Packard on Model 2-35 Twin-six. One portion of roof above rear quarter window was hinged to swing forward above door section.

Catalogue drawing of the Limousine-Landaulet on Model 2-35, which sold for $4,765 in 1916.

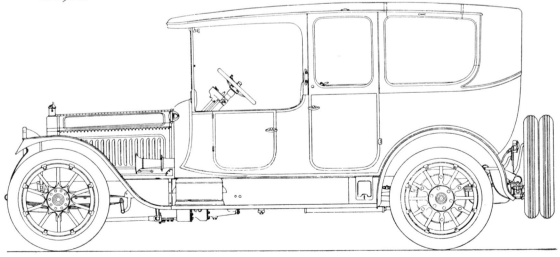

An Imperial Limousine of 1916. The rear section is similar to Miss Held's car, but the chauffeur's compartment is completely enclosed.

By 1917, the scuttle had been smoothed, but much of the body is very similar to earlier ones.

After buying bodies from outside sources for some years, Packard revived its Custom Body Division for the 1929 Speedster series. This Roadster is identified as Model X-126, and its body is a shortened version of the standard Roadster. A limited number were offered at $5,000.

For 1930, a revised Speedster in several styles on Model 734 was available, the most popular being the Boat-tailed Roadster shown here at an auto show.

A restored Model 734 Speedster Roadster owned by Mr. George Jepson of Hillsdale, New Jersey.

Another restored Model 734 Speedster Roadster belonging to Harrah's Automobile Collection, Reno, Nevada.

Another body style on the Model 734
Speedster chassis was the Phaeton. The
Packard bodyplate is clearly visible.

A nicely restored Speedster Phaeton with its
owner, Mr. George Jepson of Hillsdale,
New Jersey, at the wheel.

Packard files identify this only as a special Sedan for Mr. Macaulay on Model 845. It was probably built by the newly revived Custom Body Division.

The Packard stand at the 1931 New York Auto Show included the All-weather Sport Cabriolet at left, with body from Packard Custom Body Division. At right is a late type Waterhouse Convertible Victoria.

Packard's Style No. 3008 All-weather Cabriolet on Model 840 of 1931 sold for $5,750.

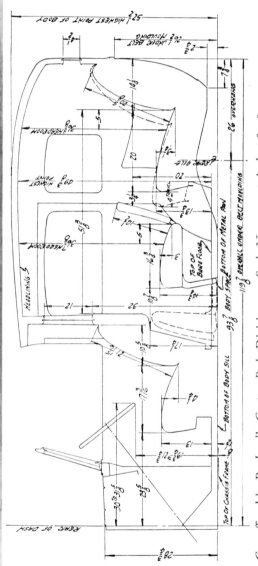

The largest Town Car offered by Packard's Custom Body Division was Style No. 3002 priced at $5,875. Interior dimensions of Packard's Style No. 3002 Town Car and its companion Style No. 3003 Landaulet, which sold for $6,075.

Actually the same size as the Town Car although looking smaller with its closed rear quarters, Style No. 3000 All-weather Cabriolet sold for $5,750.

The same basic styles were offered for 1932, but on the longest wheelbase with somewhat more interior room and higher prices. This is the interior of Model No. 4009 Landaulet which sold for $7,550 on Model 906 Twelve.

The larger Model 4003 Landaulet had also increased in size and price, up to $7,950 on Model 906 Twelve.

Another Packard Custom model was Style No. 4004 Cabriolet Sedan-Limousine with closed front. In 1932 it sold for $6,850 on Model 904 Eight or $7,550 on Model 906 Twelve. The other Packard Custom bodies were also available on either chassis, but most were ordered on the Twelve.

By 1933 some further changes had been made. This Town Car carried the same Style Number, 4002, as the year before and was unchanged in size but somewhat more rounded, and less expensive at $6,080 on Model 1006 Twelve.

A special Speedster for Mr. Edward Macaulay, which he had designed, on a 1933 chassis. The rear of the body is very much like those in the earlier Model 734 Speedsters, but the long bonnet, special mudguards and Vee windscreen change its appearance considerably.

This special Coupé on a 1934 chassis was also designed by Edward Macaulay and credited to the Packard Custom Body Division, but was actually built at the LeBaron-Detroit plant, who also made some other versions.

CHAPTER THREE

Brewster

James Brewster established a carriage factory in New York City in 1810, and his descendants continued the business for more than a century. By the time the automobile age dawned, they were already the oldest and possibly the best carriage builders in the United States. Soon their customers turned to them to build bodies for their new cars, just as they had earlier bought their Broughams and Victorias from Brewster. It took some time to convince William Brewster, however, that the automobile was here to stay, and their first motor car body was not built until 1905.

Unlike most American coachbuilders, Brewster preferred to sell complete automobiles. Before World War I they imported Delaunay-Belleville and Rolls-Royce chassis, which they fitted with luxurious coachwork. When the war cut off their supply of such chassis, they manufactured their own car for some years. At the same time, they would not refuse a commission to build a body on some other chassis. A few Packards were among these.

After the Rolls-Royce Company of America was formed in 1921, their source of this fine chassis was cut off, as the new company insisted on marketing the cars themselves. While still selling some of the smaller Brewster cars, the firm became agents for both Marmon and Packard. They sold these chassis only with Brewster bodies, leaving the business on production models to others. The Brewster showroom now was at Fifth Avenue and 56th Street in New York, and usually had at least one or two Brewster Packards on display.

At the end of 1925, Rolls-Royce and Brewster had made up their differences, and the two firms were merged. This ended the arrangement with Packard for a time. However, the market crash of 1929 brought them together again. Brewster designed some attractive new bodies for the Packard chassis, which were ordered in lots of 5 at a time by the New York branch, but actually were available through all Packard dealers.

The declining market for expensive cars forced Brewster along with the American Rolls-Royce into receivership in 1931. However, they continued to operate under court supervision until 1938, and turned out an occasional coachbuilt Packard.

When the company was finally liquidated in 1938, John Inskip took over much of their assets and became American agent for Rolls-Royce. A few additional bodies were built in the Brewster plant under the Inskip name, including one or two for Packards.

One of the new series of Brewster bodies on Model 745-C, introduced for 1930, this Convertible Sedan sold for $7,005.

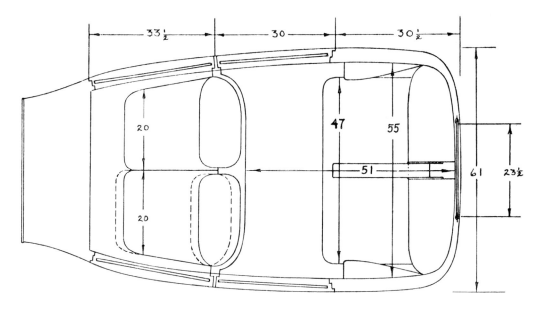

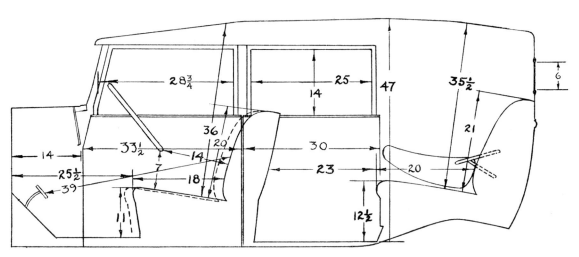

Interior dimensions of Style 7815 Convertible Sedan.

Another Brewster body for 1930, Style No. 7813 Sedan-Limousine sold for $7,260 on Model 745-C.

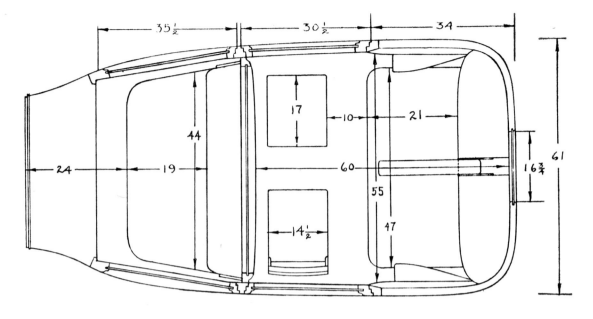

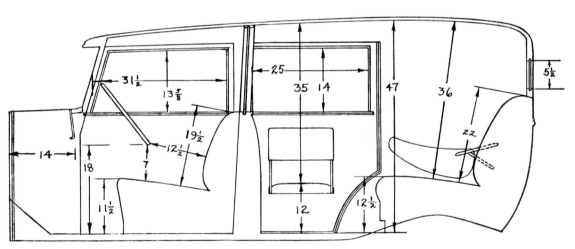

Interior dimensions of Style No. 7813 Sedan-Limousine.

Brewster's Style No. 7936 Sedan-Limousine was similar but had rear quarter windows.

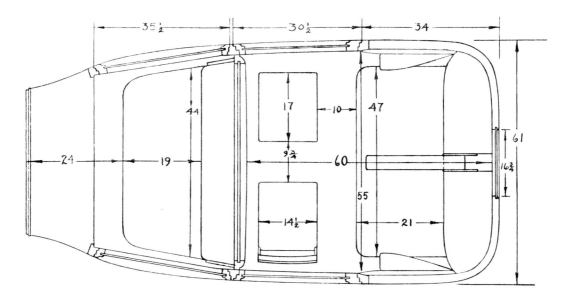

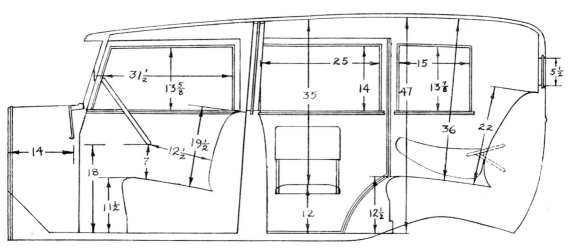

Interior dimensions of Style No. 7936 Sedan-Limousine, which sold for $7,435.

This All-weather Cabriolet type of town car, Style No. 7812, sold for $7,255 on Model 745-C.

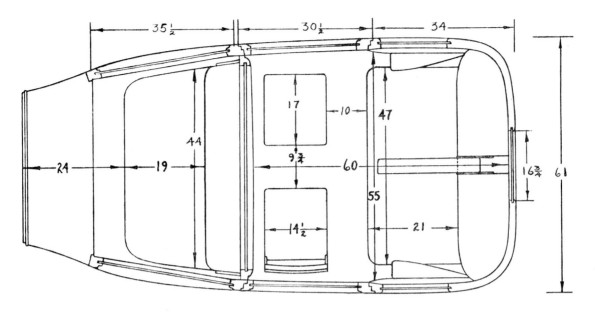

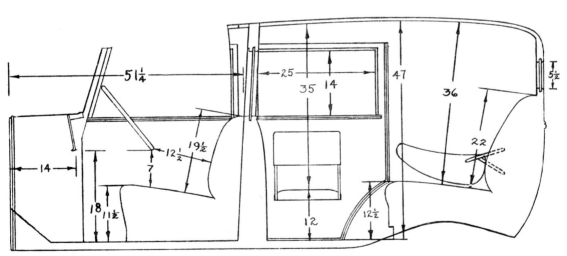

Interior dimensions of Style No. 7812 Cabriolet.

The All-weather Landaulet, Style No. 7934, was similar to the Cabriolet except for its folding roof, but cost $7,595.

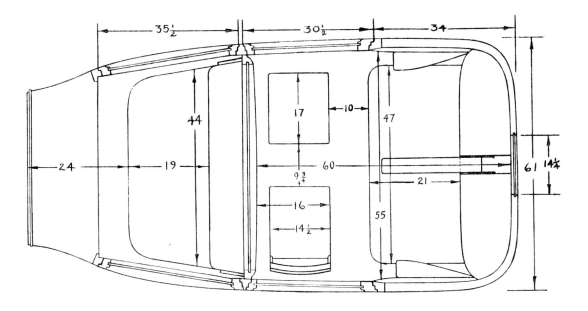

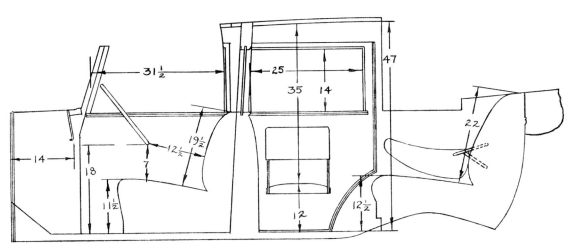

Interior dimensions of Style No. 7934 Landaulet.

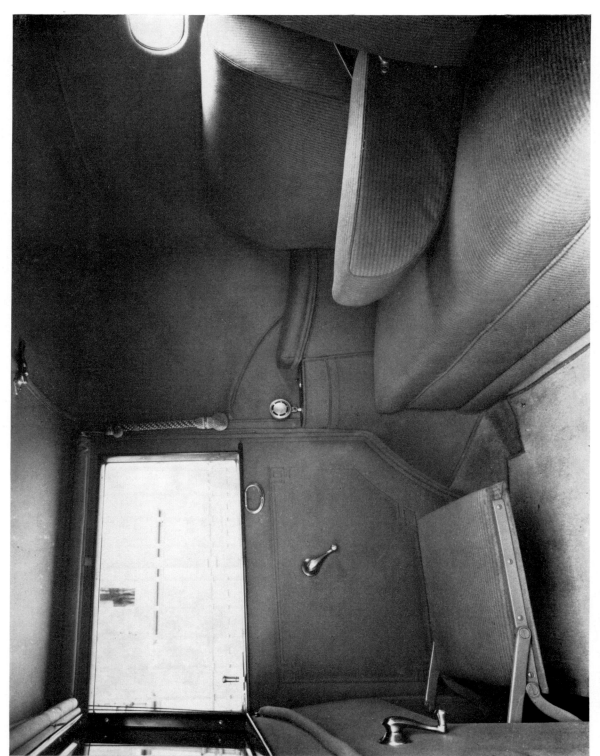

Packard's files identify this only as a special Club Sedan for Mr. Macaulay, but many details are very similar to the bodies Brewster built in small series for Packard, and the special bumpers are almost identical with those Brewster was using on Rolls-Royces at this time.

Brewster in the mid-thirties built similar Town Broughams on several chassis including modified Fords. While those Fords and some others had special heart-shaped radiators, Brewster retained the Packard radiator for those mounted on special longer-wheelbase Model 120.

A Brewster Panel Brougham originally built in 1911 on a Delaunay-Belleville chassis but remounted by Brewster on a Packard 120 in 1936. The present owner is Mr. H. Charles Riker of Huntington, New York.

Since its original owner wished to preserve the general appearance of the car as first built, the Packard radiator was replaced with one as used on Brewster cars of the late teens, which was similar to that of the Delaunay-Belleville. A new bonnet and scuttle were made to match. The rear view of the Brewster Brougham shows the leather mudguards as used originally.

CHAPTER FOUR

Darrin

A young pilot during World War I, Howard A. "Dutch" Darrin met Thomas L. Hibbard while serving in France. In 1923 the two young men returned to Paris to check on having bodies built there to the designs of LeBaron, which Hibbard had helped found, but instead set up their own new firm of Hibbard & Darrin. Initially they too, designed bodies and had them built by various coachbuilders, but eventually they established their own factory in a Paris suburb.

The stock market crash of 1929 was a crisis for their financial backer, and the firm closed its doors the next year. While Hibbard returned to the United States, Darrin formed a new partnership with a wealthy furniture manufacturer, as Fernandez & Darrin. By 1937, Darrin, too, was back in America and settled in Hollywood whose movie colony would hopefully provide a market for coachbuilt cars.

His first experiments there were on Packard 120 chassis, fitted with bodies of distinctly European appearance. Some orders resulted, but they also attracted the attention of Packard management. This placed Darrin in a quandary, since his Hollywood shop was not large enough to turn out any large quantity of bodies.

Arrangements were made to have them built by the Central Manufacturing Company in Indiana, and for several years Darrin travelled back and forth, working out new ideas in Hollywood and supervising the construction of bodies of his design in Indiana. When the Central Manufacturing Company became fully occupied with building Jeep bodies, the work for Darrin was transferred to the Hess & Eisenhart shop in Cincinnati, and the last Darrin Packards came from there.

The bodies actually built by these two firms under Darrin's supervision were of course the Convertible Victorias, low four-seaters with folding roofs and windows in the doors. Darrin continued to build a few other types on special order in his own shop in California.

An early Darrin Convertible Victoria on Model 180, photographed in 1939. It sold for $4,570 on 127-inch wheelbase.

Many people think the Darrin Convertible looked best with the top folded, as in this view.

Slight differences mark this 1941 version by Darrin. The car is owned by Mr. Ken Hinds of Glen Burnie, Maryland.

Darrin himself modified this body into a Coupé de Ville, with fixed roof over the rear seat.

A four-door Convertible Sedan by Darrin on a 1940 Model 180 of the longer 138-inch wheelbase, which sold for $6,300.

One of the Darrin Sport Sedans as shown in a catalogue for the 1941 Model 180. The car sold for $4,795 on 138-inch wheelbase.

A 1941 Darrin Model 180 Convertible Victoria, owned by Mr. Patrick G. Young of Tilton, New Hampshire.

CHAPTER FIVE

Derham Body Company

Founded as a carriage-builder in Philadelphia in 1887, this firm continued under ownership by the Derham family until just a few years ago. Like some other already established coachbuilders, they were approached by their clients to build bodies for their new automobiles and soon found it necessary to move to larger quarters. A modern building was erected in suburban Rosemont, near the area where many of their wealthy customers lived.

Besides dealing directly with individual customers, Derham also worked closely with the local agents for various expensive cars, especially the Packard distributor there. They also sought business more widely, and obtained many orders from Mr. Parvis when he was handling custom body purchases for the Packard branch in New York.

During their earlier period as coachbuilders for automobiles, a large proportion of Derham's bodies were the more formal chauffeur-driven types. Occasionally, they would produce a more sporting coupé or phaeton. By the late 'twenties, they had become adept at fashioning attractive convertible bodies, a type that was to be more in demand during the succeeding Depression days. However, they still turned out some town broughams even in that period.

With the reduced demand, the cost of building completely individual formal bodies became prohibitively high, one factor that forced the closing of many of their competitors. Derham worked to solve this by developing methods of altering or modifying a standard sedan body into a limousine, changing its appearance with the substitution of a softly padded top or one of different shape, while retaining a substantial portion of the structure of the standard body.

They created convertible sedans in much the same manner, using the lower portion of the standard sedan. Such modifications could be done at lower cost than building a complete body, and kept Derham in business during the late Depression years and in fact on into the postwar period.

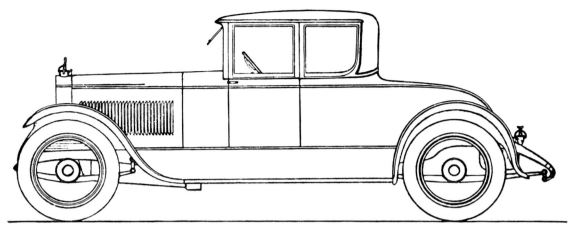

From a brochure illustrating Packards to be shown at the October, 1921, New York Salon comes this drawing of a Derham Coupé on Model 3-35 Twin-six.

Another Derham body at that 1921 Salon was this Inside Drive Sedan, also on Model 3-35 Twin-six.

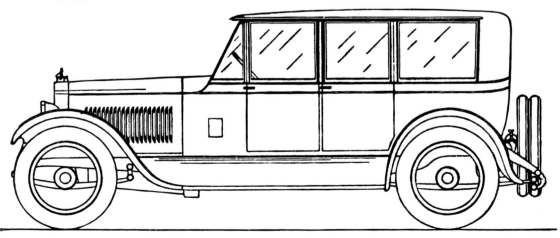

A Stationary Cabriolet type of Town Car on Model 143 Eight, displayed at the 1924 New York Salon.

Packard's Custom Body Catalogue for the Model 243 Eight included this dimension drawing of Style No. 3509 Derham Cabriolet, very similar to the preceding photograph.

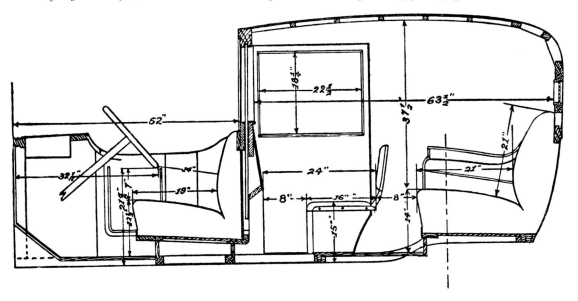

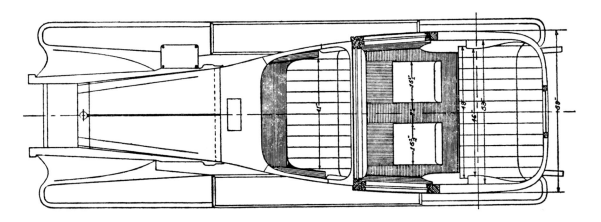

A Glass-quarter Brougham on Model 143 Eight of 1924.

A somewhat later Brougham on Model 443, probably from late 1927.

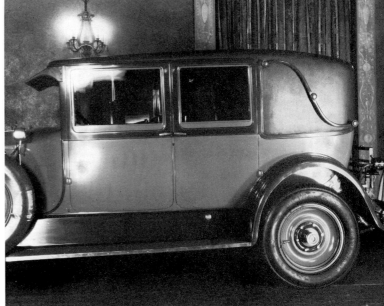

Derham's advertisement in the catalogue for the 1925 New York Salon featured this Sedan-Limousine on Model 243 Eight

The following year Derham showed a similar Sedan-Limousine at the Salon, on Model 343 Eight.

A Sport Sedan on Model 443, photographed new in late 1927.

Derham built this Convertible Coupé on the smaller Model 533 chassis. Note the forward slope of rear portion of top.

By 1930, Derham had designed this rakish Convertible Coupé, several of which were built on Model 745 Eights, and sold for $6,485.

A Town Brougham of 1936 on Model 120. The coachlamps and special mudguards are reminiscent of an earlier age.

This Town Car on a 1937 Model 120 seems to have been modified from a standard sedan.

There were still occasional orders for very formal Panel Broughams such as this one which Derham built in 1938, reputedly for opera singer Lily Pons.

Open tourers were no longer being offered as standard models when Derham built this one on a Model 1608 Twelve of 1938.

The Tourer with top folded.

Derham rebuilt this 1938 Model 1608 Twelve Limousine for Mr. W. H. Luden, the cough-drop man. He was unhappy with the sunroof, so had Derham add a windshield for it later. The car is now owned by Mr. George Isbell of Memphis, Tennessee.

By 1939, much of Derham's work was modifying standard bodies such as this Twelve Formal Sedan which they made into a Limousine with padded roof. It is now owned by Mr. William Deibel of Detroit.

CHAPTER SIX

Dietrich

The name of Dietrich is always closely linked to coachbuilt Packards of the late 'twenties and early 'thirties, partly because many carried this nameplate, and also, since many of them were the more sporting types, a high proportion of them survive.

Raymond Henri Dietrich started his career as an apprentice draughtsman with Brewster & Company and went on to found LeBaron with his co-worker Thomas L. Hibbard. He left that firm in the spring of 1925 to set up his own custom-body firm in Detroit with financial backing from the Murray Corporation. At the time, the latter was a newly formed merger of several independent body builders who numbered Lincoln and Packard among their better customers. Edsel Ford had been instrumental in persuading Dietrich to add his name to the group, but before long Packard became his largest customer.

When the Dietrich factory was first set up in Detroit, many of the bodies bore a strong resemblance to designs he had conceived for LeBaron. Soon he developed some new ideas in convertible bodies and these became a major portion of his work, although he still turned out some town cars, limousines and other more formal types.

With the onset of the Depression, some differences on policy developed and Ray Dietrich left the firm, but it was continued as a subsidiary of Murray for a few years. Many of the bodies from this period had been designed by Dietrich or bore traces of his influence. Others, using his ideas, were adapted to standard Packard bodies built at the Murray plant.

After Ray Dietrich left about the end of 1930, the separate plant occupied by the firm was closed, and production of Dietrich bodies transferred to the Murray plant. By 1933, some of the earlier Dietrich designs or adaptations of them had become the standard Packard convertible models. Bodies of the same design but with more elaborate interior finish were made alongside the standard models, and carried the Dietrich nameplate and of course a higher price.

This arrangement continued through 1936, when the last Dietrich bodies were completed. Actually a few were mounted on 1937 chassis, introduced towards the end of that year.

Ray Dietrich himself continued for some years as an employee of or consultant to various automobile companies.

The Packard stand at the New York Auto Show in January, 1926, featured a Dietrich Convertible Coupé, introduced a few months before as one of their first Packards.

Interior dimensions of the Convertible Coupé on Model 243 Eight, Style No. 1222.

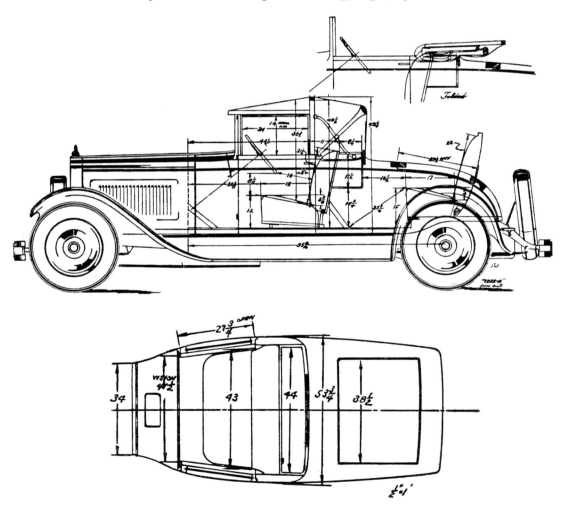

Another model was this Club Sedan on Model 243, a close-coupled four-passenger body. Some of its styling influenced later Packards.

Interior dimensions of the Club Sedan, Style No. 1176, from a Packard custom body brochure issued in late 1925.

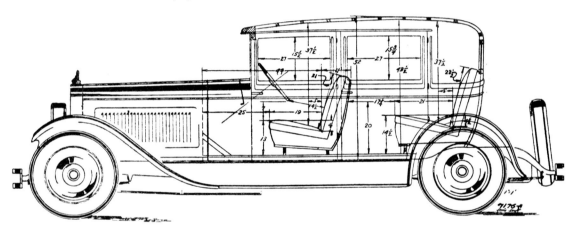

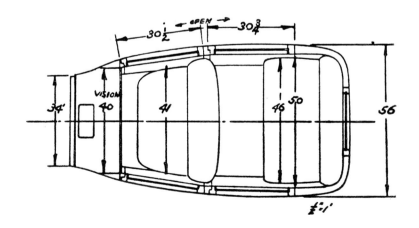

Dietrich also built some town cars. This Cabriolet on Model 243 was one of his earliest.

Interior dimensions of Style No. 1177 Stationary Town Cabriolet.

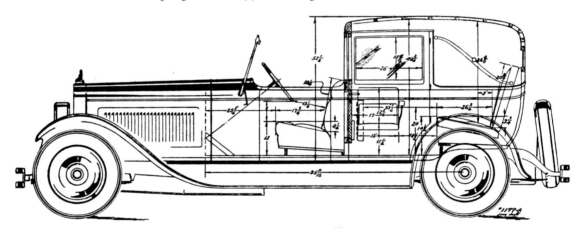

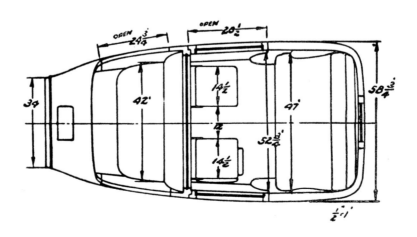

Custom bodies bought in series by Packard were available at this time on the Model 333 Six as well as the larger Eight. This is a Dietrich Town Cabriolet on the smaller chassis.

By the time Model 343 was introduced in the Autumn of 1926, Dietrich was following the trend to "All-weather" Town Cars with windows in the front doors in place of side curtains.

A full seven-passenger All-weather Town Brougham on Model 443 Eight for 1928.

A later All-weather Town Cabriolet on Model 443, with opera seating as on Style No. 1177.

Packard used the Dietrich Town Cabriolet to illustrate its advertisements. This shows the canopy over the chauffeur in place.

By *1928* Dietrich's Convertible Coupé design had been modified somewhat and the outside landau irons eliminated.
Similar in some respects to the Convertible, this Coupé has a fixed roof, and retains the purely decorative landau irons. It is also on Model *443* Eight.

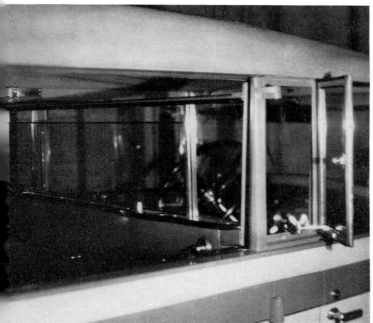

At the *1927* New York Salon, Dietrich introduced this Convertible Sedan on Model 443 Eight, with vent windows between the doors. This illustration is from Dietrich's advertisement in the Salon catalogue.

This photograph taken at Dietrich's Salon stand shows the vent window open. One can also see the partition window, making it really a Convertible Sedan-Limousine.

Packards' own advertisement in the Salon catalogue had a different illustration of a similar Convertible Sedan.

For the Model 640 chassis, Dietrich continued the same basic design of Convertible Sedan.

A new style for Model 640 was the Convertible Victoria. These early ones had windows in the rear quarters.

The Convertible Victoria was quite attractive with top folded. It sold for $7,064.

An experimental Convertible Victoria with some subtle differences in design. This was "trial mounted" in the Packard factory which accounts for the contrasting hood colour, not a usual colour scheme.

Early Dietrich Victorias had folding rear seats, which could be swung out of the way when extra luggage space was needed with only two passengers.

Below: *For the later Model 645, Dietrich redesigned the Convertible Sedan using a sloping windscreen as on the Victoria, and eliminating the centre vent window.*

Dietrich also revised the design of his Convertible Coupé to use the sloping windscreen.

In redesigning his Convertible Coupé, Dietrich lowered the rear deck, which in turn permitted the top to fold more attractively.

Another body style added for the 645 chassis was this Sport Phaeton.

An experimental Convertible Victoria on a Model 633 chassis had closed rear quarters and a different moulding treatment below the doors.

Town cars were still coming from the Dietrich factory, and this Model 645 Town Brougham was an individual design.

Interior of the Town Brougham.

An experimental idea was this "Peter Jones Observation Car," modified at the Dietrich plant from a standard Sedan-Limousine. Jones was an Englishman who patented the idea and had some bodies built in England before interesting Packard. Note how windows almost completely surround the body.

The Peter Jones design had a door in the rear panel, and the rear seat itself could be reversed to face backward. The idea did not catch the public fancy.

An All-weather Town Cabriolet on the smaller Model 633 Eight.

The Packard display at the 1930 New York Auto Show featured a Dietrich Dual-cowl Phaeton on Model 745.

Dietrich's Convertible Sedan on Model 745, Style No. 1602, continued the basic design he had introduced on the previous model.

Interior of Style No. 1602 Convertible Sedan.

A nicely restored Model 745 Convertible Sedan.

Interior dimensions of Style No. 1602 Convertible Sedan, which sold for $6,795 on Model 745.

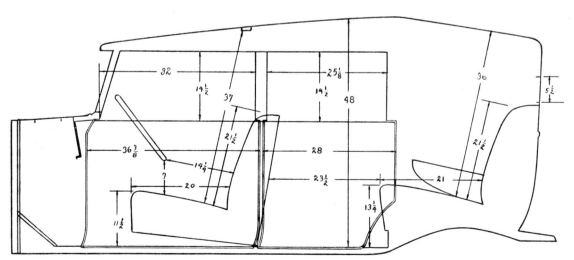

The Convertible Sedan on Model 840 for 1931, Style No. 1881, was little changed except in price, which was reduced to $5,275.

A restored Model 840 Dietrich Convertible Sedan, owned by Harrah's Automobile Collection, Reno, Nevada.

Important style notes are the seating arrangement, trunk location, tailored trim and folding arm rest

The top folds low to carry out the smooth sweep of graceful body design from radiator tip to rear lines

THE DIETRICH CONVERTIBLE VICTORIA
Four Places

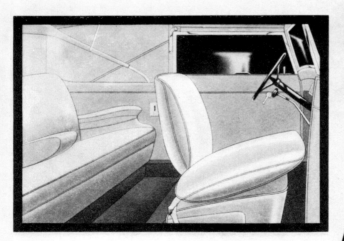

A BRILLIANT design in any scene is this low-lined sport type with the appearance of a Coupe or Roadster at will. Yet full comfort for four passengers is afforded by placing the rear seat forward and artfully recessing the floor just behind the front seats. A trunk is mounted on the back for tools, top boot and luggage. The driver's seat is adjustable and the other folds for easy entrance or egress from the rear seat

Convenient vanity and smoking sets fit flush into the body wall in neat recesses, with a push type cigar lighter placed above the smoking set

A catalogue page showing exterior and interior views of Dietrich's Style No. 1879 Convertible Victoria on Model 840, which sold for $5,175.

A special Sport Sedan by Dietrich on Model 845, which incorporated some of the ideas used on his bodies for the 9th Series. The car is now owned by Harrah's Automobile Collection, Reno, Nevada.

Dietrich's Stationary Coupé, Style No. 2068, had lines very similar to the Convertible.

Interior dimensions of Style No. 2068 Coupé, which sold for $5,900 on Model 904 Eight or $6,600 on Model 906 Twin-six.

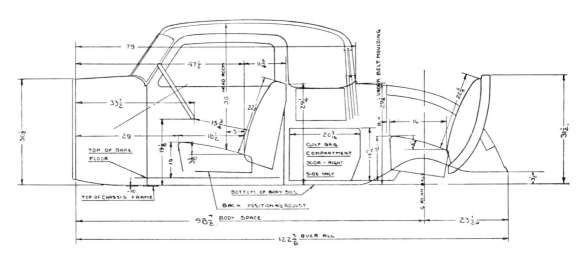

*Interior and exterior views of a
Style No. 2070 Convertible Sedan on
Model 906 Twin-six, and below are
the interior dimensions of the
Convertible Sedan, which sold for $6,250 on
Model 904 Eight or $6,950 on Model 906
Twin-six.*

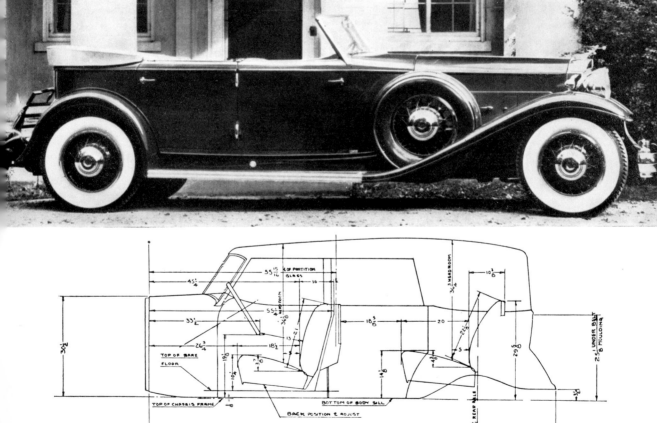

A 1932 Sport Phaeton by Dietrich at a meet. The side panels of the tonneau windscreen could be folded inwards, and the whole unit lowered into the body.

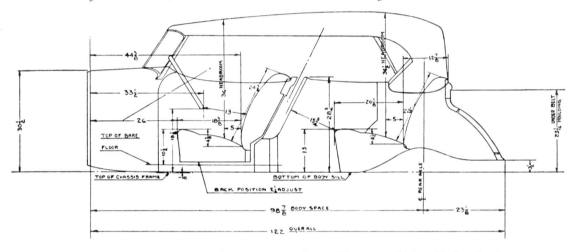

Interior dimensions of the Style No. 2069 Sport Phaeton, which sold for $5,800 on Model 904 Eight or $6,500 on Model 906 Twin-six.

Another Dietrich Sport Phaeton, showing the small boot at rear, not big enough for luggage but convenient for small odds and ends.

A Convertible Sedan with chauffeur's partition and 3-position top to make it usable as a Town Car. This is on a Model 902 chassis, and is owned by Mr. Lars Kile, Jr., of Christianssand, Norway.

By 1933, Dietrich and Murray bodies were being built side by side and differed only in details. This Convertible Victoria owned by David Steinman of Gwynedd Valley, Pennsylvania, has all the features of the Dietrich model but for some reason the factory identified it as a production body.

A Convertible Sedan on Model 1006 Twelve of 1933, owned by Mr. Shelley D. Vincent of Mendon, Massachusetts.

A similar Convertible Sedan owned by Mr. Streeter B. Flynn, Jr., of Oklahoma City, Oklahoma.

Dietrich built this Sport Limousine for display at the 1933 Chicago World's Fair. There was a chauffeur's partition although the rear compartment would seat only two people.

The World's Fair car attracted so much attention that some duplicate bodies were built for the 1934 Twelve.

Catalogue rendering of a Convertible Sedan on Model 1108 Twelve for 1934.

The rendering was very close to the appearance of the actual car, photographed when new.

A Convertible Sedan on Model 1107 Twelve of 1934, following earlier styling but fitted with chauffeur's partition and other special features. The car is owned by Mr. Jerry W. Jones of Indianapolis, Indiana.

Another Convertible Victoria on a 1935 Super Eight.

Dietrich built this special seven-passenger Touring Car on a 1935 Twelve for use in parades by President Franklin D. Roosevelt.

One of the last Dietrich bodies is this Convertible Victoria, left unsold at the end of 1936 production and so mounted on a 1937 chassis. It is owned by Mr. Andrew Henderson of Grosse Pointe, Michigan.

CHAPTER SEVEN

Fleetwood

For forty years or more, this subsidiary of General Motors has been known as the Fleetwood Division of the Fisher Body Company, and closely identified with Cadillac. However, prior to its purchase by the Fisher brothers in 1925, it was an independent coachbuilding firm whose principal customer had been Packard.

Founded in 1905 as the Reading Metal Body Company in Reading, Pennsylvania, the firm set up a branch plant in nearby Fleetwood which soon became its headquarters. In 1911 the name was changed to Fleetwood Metal Body Company.

With the introduction of the Twin Six, Fleetwood began to turn out an increasing number of bodies for this chassis. Early Packard custom body catalogues show more Fleetwood bodies than any others. The close connection continued after the introduction of the Packard Eight, right up to the time that Fleetwood became part of Fisher in 1925.

Even after that, some Fleetwood bodies were mounted on Packards, including some small series of town cars. The last came on the Series 443 chassis for the 1927/8 model year, one of which was displayed on the Fleetwood stand at the New York Automobile Salon late in 1927.

Earlier Fleetwood Packards had run the gamut from open two-seater runabouts to elegant limousines and town cars. Some of the open cars were quite dashing in appearance and some elements of their styling were carried over into Packard production bodies of the early 'twenties.

In 1929, General Motors built a new Fleetwood body plant in Detroit, and by 1931 the earlier one in Pennsylvania had closed. Thereafter only Cadillacs appeared with Fleetwood bodies, except for a few on its sister LaSalle in the 'thirties.

This Cabriolet was built in 1918 especially for an aunt of Phil Hill, in whose collection in Santa Monica, California, it now resides. Original cost was $9,000.

Another view of Mr. Hill's Fleetwood Cabriolet. The decorative panel below the rear window is painted canework.

Packard's files called this 1919 Twin-six an "experimental body," but it is obviously a Fleetwood Runabout.

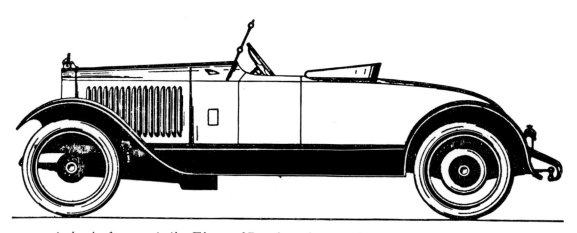

A sketch of a very similar Fleetwood Runabout shown at the 1921 New York Salon, from a brochure prepared by Packard's New York branch on that occasion.

A Fleetwood Cabriolet on special long wheelbase. It has much the effect of the later Eight, but was built two years before the car illustrated on the next page was introduced.

This Cabriolet, photographed at the 1920 New York Salon, was on a lengthened chassis of 143-inch wheelbase, with special long bonnet.

A Phaeton built for actress Marylin Miller on a 1920 Twin-six. Note special luggage fitted to running boards and front bumper.

The brochure of drawings of cars exhibited at the 1921 Salon included these two Fleetwood Touring Cars, the smaller of which is quite similar to Miss Miller's.

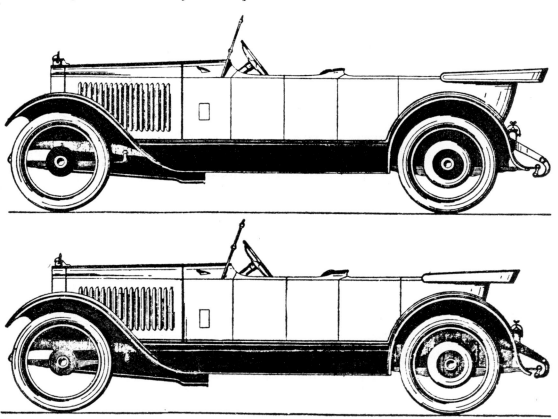

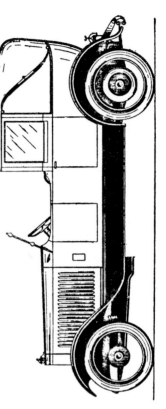

A drawing of another Fleetwood Packard at that 1921 Salon was this Town Cabriolet.

The Packard showroom in New York about 1921 or 1922 with a Fleetwood Town Cabriolet at left and what seem to be two more Coachbuilt Packards in the far end.

A Limousine on a late Twin-six of 1922. The twin ventilators in the roof were characteristic of many Fleetwood bodies.

A Sport Sedan, photographed at the 1922 New York Salon. This appears to have been specially built for that display.

A Glass-quarter Brougham on an early Model 143 Eight.

A rendering of a Fleetwood Phaeton on Model 143 Eight. The basic design continues much like their previous bodies of this type on the Twin-six.

A completely different Phaeton, also from 1924. The high body sides were deliberately planned to protect passengers from wind in high-speed touring.

Another Fleetwood Phaeton on Model 243 Eight has rounded lines quite different from their earlier open bodies.

A Town Cabriolet with special six-mudguard equipment, built for actress Hope Hampton in 1925.
The basic body for Miss Hampton was Fleetwood's Style No. 1509 Town Cabriolet, whose interior dimensions are shown here.

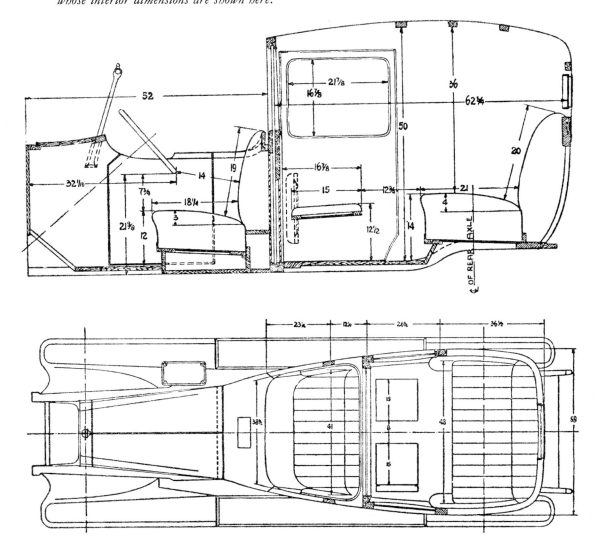

Fleetwood built several Sedan-Limousines such as this on Model 243 Eight.

At the 1926 New York Salon, Fleetwood showed this Town Brougham of very similar design to an Isotta-Fraschini they had displayed earlier and which was purchased by Rudolph Valentino.

One of the last Fleetwood Packards was this Town Car displayed on a Model 443 chassis at the 1927 New York Salon.

CHAPTER EIGHT

Holbrook

Founded by Harry F. Holbrook and John D. Graham in 1908 to build custom automobile bodies, this firm started in New York City which had not only wealthy clients, but many skilled craftsmen who had learned their trade in carriage days. By 1913, Harry Holbrook left the company which bore his name, and it was operated thereafter by Jack Graham. About this time, too, Packard became a leading customer.

Having outgrown their original shop on the west side of New York, they added another about a mile away. This was a somewhat awkward arrangement since part of the work on each body was done in one shop, and the balance in the other. In 1921, Holbrook found a suitable location in Hudson, New York, 100 miles up the river of that name, and moved their factory there.

They maintained a close relationship with Mr. Parvis at the Packard branch in New York, and much of their business came from this source. The bodies included town cars and limousines, but in 1925 the Packard factory ordered a series of coupés of which 100 or so were built. Holbrook also built some striking phaetons for display at the Automobile Salons.

The financial backing of the firm had come from some wealthy New York garment manufacturers. Unfortunately they were hard hit by the 1929 stock market crash, and by May of the following year Holbrook was forced into bankruptcy. Some of their assets were purchased by Rollston, and several of Holbrook's staff joined that company.

Just prior to this, they had become licensees for Gordon England's patent light-weight body, and there was even talk of merger with his firm. Unfortunately the financial crash prevented this. The Gordon England licence was among Holbrook assets acquired by Rollston, but no bodies of this type were actually built.

For a 1917 exhibit, Holbrook built this Full-collapsible Cabriolet with special six-mudguard equipment and rounded scuttle.

By 1921, Holbrook was turning out a series of these Enclosed-drive Limousines for Packard.

Packard's files identify this only as a "Special Limousine" on a 1920 Twin-six. Various details are close to the design of the Holbrook Limousines.

A Holbrook Town Cabriolet on a 1921 Twin-six, with very angular lines even in the landau irons.

Photographed in 1920, this Holbrook Twin-six Limousine was different from an earlier Style No. 806.

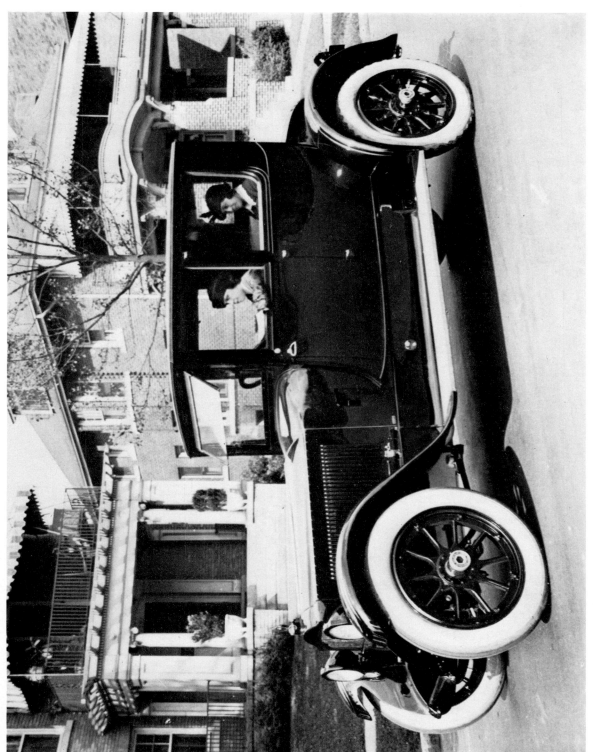

Holbrook built other styles than town cars, such as this four-passenger Coupé on a 1919 Twin-six.

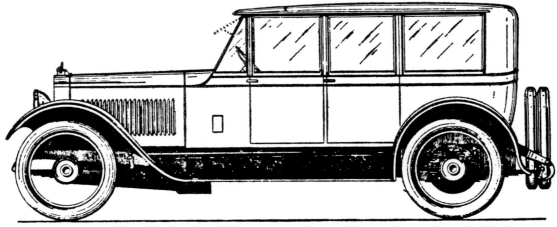

At the *1921* New York Salon, Holbrook showed several Packards including this "Inside Drive Limousine," similar to one in an earlier photograph.

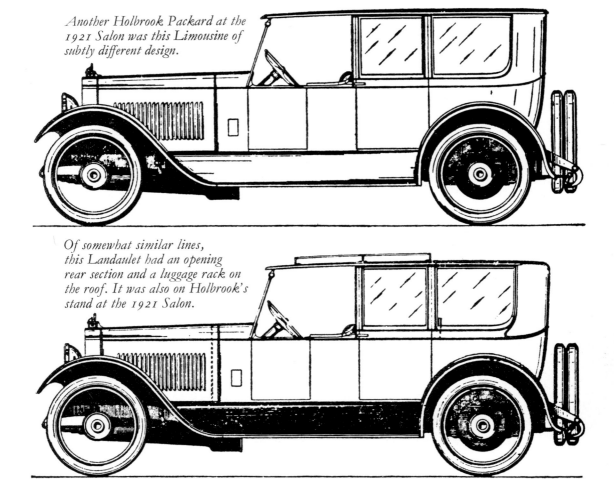

Another Holbrook Packard at the 1921 Salon was this Limousine of subtly different design.

Of somewhat similar lines, this Landaulet had an opening rear section and a luggage rack on the roof. It was also on Holbrook's stand at the 1921 Salon.

Rakish for its time, Holbrook showed this Sport Sedan on the new Model 143 Eight at the 1923 New York Salon.

A more individual Packard is this Holbrook Panel Brougham, sketched by Laurence Fellows for Vanity Fair. *It is on a six-cylinder chassis.*

Holbrook's President John Graham had this Coupé built on a 1922 Twin-six for his own use.

Opera singer Mme. Alda commissioned this Town Brougham, also on a 1922 Twin-six, with rather square lines.

Holbrook had a flair for Phaetons and this one on a 1922 Twin-six looks unusually low for its time.

This Twin-six Cabriolet was built by Holbrook in 1922 for Hon. James W. Gerard, America's Ambassador to France.

A restored Holbrook Enclosed-drive Limousine of 1924 photographed at a meet in Stowe, Vermont, in 1960.

Interior dimensions of Holbrook's Style No. 2711 Enclosed-drive Limousine, from a 1925 Packard custom body brochure.

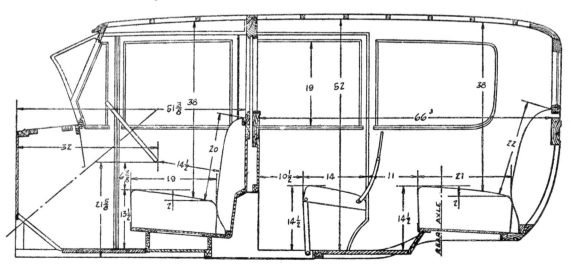

One of Holbrook's most successful designs, *100 or more of these Coupés were built, beginning
in mid-1925 on Model 236. This one was photographed new.*

*Interior dimensions of Holbrook's Style No. 653 Coupé, which could also be ordered on
Model 326 Six.*

One of two surviving Holbrook Coupés belongs to Mr. James Silvey of Indianapolis, Indiana.

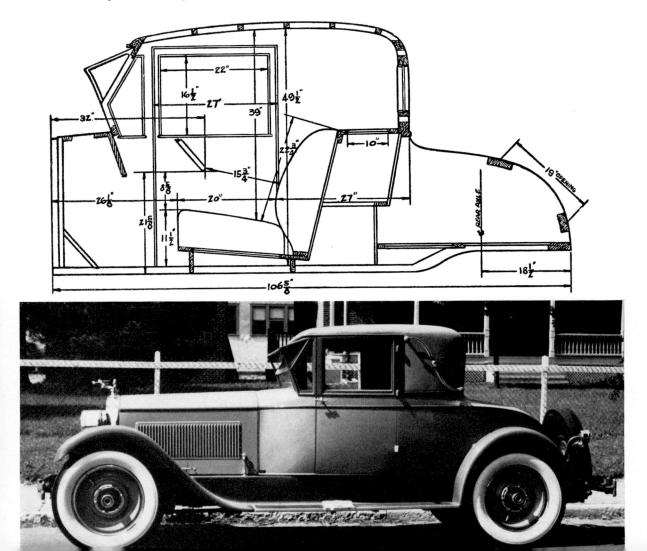

The Holbrook stand at the 1926 New York Salon included this Town Brougham on Model 343 Eight.

A later version of Holbrook's Enclosed-drive Limousine is this on a 1928 Model 443 Eight.

One of the most striking Phaetons Holbrook ever built, with lavish use of polished aluminium, dazzled the eyes of visitors to the 1927 New York Salon where it was shown on a Model 443 Eight.

Another later Holbrook body, Style No. 921 All-weather Cabriolet, also on Model 443.

CHAPTER NINE

John B. Judkins

Amesbury, Massachusetts, some fifty miles north of Boston, was an early carriage-building centre in America, so much so that one part of town became known as "Carriage Hill" because many of the shops were located there.

In 1857 John B. Judkins and Isaac Little set up a partnership in West Amesbury as coachbuilders. Over the years, the firm changed to Judkins & Goodwin, then Judkins & Haskell. In 1883, Frederick Judkins, son of the founder, joined the company which became John B. Judkins & Son. When another son was admitted to the firm, it was known as J. B. Judkins & Sons Company. After its founder's death in 1908, the name was changed again to The John B. Judkins Company, which it retained for the balance of its career. The town, too, had changed its name and was now known as Merrimac, after the river which furnished water power for its early factories.

Judkins built their first automobile bodies in the 1890s, and had already acquired considerable experience in this field when Alvan T. Fuller, the Packard distributor in Boston, began purchasing special bodies from them for his new Twin Sixes. Judkins continued to turn out a variety of Packard bodies into the mid-twenties. By then, they began getting substantial orders from Lincoln for their coupés and berlines, and were less active on other chassis.

During the Depression years, they still built a fair number of Lincolns and an occasional body on Packard or other chassis. To keep the plant busy, they turned to making trailers for sales and demonstration purposes. In 1938 they turned out their last coachbuilt body, and by 1941 the trailer business was also discontinued and the company liquidated. John B. Judkins, grandson and namesake of the founder, who had run the company for the previous twenty years, later acted as a consultant to several automobile companies.

Three views of the "Grandaddy of the Hardtops". Judkins's 7-passenger "Transformable" was built in 1917 on a Model 3-35 Twin-six. With windows lowered, the posts between them could be removed and stored under the rear seats, giving maximum fresh air and visibility.

Packard's custom body catalogue for 1918
showed a similar five-passenger model on
the shorter 3-25 chassis, Style No. 532
priced at $5,050. This had only a centre
door on the driver's side.

What today would be called a "Hardtop
Coupé" was listed as a "Touring Sedan"
in 1918, somewhat less expensive at $4,800.
With its window posts removed, it looked
like this on a 1918 Twin-six.
An interior view, showing its divided bucket
seats.

A Judkins Club Sedan on 1917 Model 3-25 Twin-six, one of the earliest Packards fitted with wire wheels.

A two-passenger Coupé by Judkins on 1918 Twin-six. Square styling is reminiscent of horse-drawn carriages.

Judkins called this a "Family Sedan", with room for four. It had closed rear quarters and an unusual windscreen visor.

This dashing sedan with integral rear trunk was built in 1918 for Packard's Boston distributor, Alvan T. Fuller, who later became Governor of Massachusetts.

Judkins indicated this Coupé was built on a 1918 Twin-six, but its lines are much smoother than bodies from the early part of that year.

Judkins built this 7-passenger Limousine-Landaulet on a Model 143 Eight in 1923.

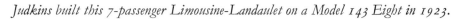

An individual body by Judkins is this 1925 "Berline-Landaulet". Judkins preferred the name "Berline" for Enclosed-drive Limousines.

The same car with rear of roof folded, and showing the interior. It was built for Mr. Walter Hinds of Portland, Maine.

At the 1927 New York Salon, Judkins showed this Sedan-Limousine on Model 443, and used a rendering to illustrate their advertisement in the Salon catalogue.

A later Judkins Sedan-Limousine on Model 645, with closed rear quarters.

CHAPTER TEN

LeBaron

Thomas L. Hibbard and Raymond H. Dietrich set up this firm in 1920 under the name of LeBaron, Carrossiers, to design and engineer automobile bodies much as architects built houses. They had met in the drawing office at Brewster & Company and each had considerable experience in the custom body field. Soon they were joined by Ralph S. Roberts, who had known Hibbard earlier, and although not himself a designer had a keen sense of style and good administrative ability.

The new group was successful in selling some designs, and the engineering drawings for many of them, but preferred to work — like architects — in supervising the construction of the bodies they designed, for a percentage fee. Such bodies were built by a number of coachbuilders in the New York area and nearby, including Demarest, Derham, Locke and others.

In the Spring of 1924, a merger was arranged with the Bridgeport Body Company in Connecticut. The new company shortened the name to LeBaron, Inc., and now had facilities for building the creations they designed. This took place a few months after the author had joined them as a sort of apprentice designer and general assistant.

Hibbard had left early in 1923 to explore the possibility of having bodies built in Europe where costs were lower, but instead wound up in partnership with Howard Darrin. In 1925, Dietrich also left to set up the company under his own name in Detroit. Other overtures came from Detroit, and by the end of 1926 LeBaron had been purchased by the Briggs Manufacturing Company there.

LeBaron was continued as a separate coachbuilding subsidiary, with added duties as the source of designs for Briggs' large customers — Ford, Graham-Paige, Chrysler and others. Roberts moved to Detroit and set up a new design centre called the LeBaron Studios, with a freshly recruited young staff, who also turned out designs for the new LeBaron-Detroit Company factory devoted largely to building custom bodies in small series.

The original operation in the East continued until the end of 1930, when reduced business prompted a consolidation of all activity in Detroit. Coachbuilt Packards and other makes continued to be built there until the beginning of the war. Following the death of Walter O. Briggs, founder of the company bearing his name, the entire body-building operation was sold to the Chrysler Corporation in 1952, they having by then become Briggs' principal client. With this went the rights to the LeBaron name, although no true coachbuilt bodies had been built under that name since just before the war.

LeBaron had designed some Packards even in their early days before they had a factory. In the mid-twenties they began turning out small series of town cars and limousines as well as many individually designed Packards. By 1930 these were joined by some convertibles, including a two-seater with top folding into the body and covered by a small boot, which had been designed by the author.

During 1931, Packard introduced custom bodies under their own name, similar to those earlier bought in small series from LeBaron. When the firm discovered that Packard were also about to introduce a coupe roadster as a standard model, very similar to the bodies they had been building, relations cooled a bit. However, by 1933 they were working again on new Packard designs, and also building some of the ideas of Edward Macaulay.

For 1934, some attractive sport models as well as more conservative town cars from LeBaron were included in Packard catalogues. Town cars and limousines by LeBaron remained a major portion of the coachbuilt Packards available until passenger car production ceased for the duration of the war.

A Convertible Sedan design by LeBaron, Carrossiers 1923. Special mudguards are similar to those on the Fairchild car.

Sedan-Limousine on Model 143 Eight, designed by LeBaron, Carrossiers, and built under their supervision by Demarest & Co. as LeBaron did not yet have a factory.

LeBaron Sedan-Limousine, Style No. 1484, of which Packard bought about 27. Introduced on Model 343, the last few were mounted on Model 443.

A Full-collapsible All-weather Cabriolet, several of which were built for Packard's Export department, on Model 443 and 645 chassis.

A later LeBaron Sedan-Limousine on Model 443 chassis, Style No. 1660. One such car was on LeBaron's stand at the 1927 New York Salon.

One of the first LeBaron All-weather Cabriolets for Model 645 was photographed in Packard's factory studio.

The illustration for this 1929 Packard ad seems to have been based on the photograph above.

The Packard stand at the 1929 New York Auto Show had a LeBaron Town Brougham (partly concealed by the pillar).

At a custom body show early in 1930, an All-weather Cabriolet and a Sedan-Limousine by LeBaron were shown (to the left of the pillars,) and just alongside them a Dietrich Convertible Victoria.

LeBaron's Style No. 1900 All-weather Cabriolet was priced at $6,885. early in 1930.

Style No. 1901 Landaulet was identical to the Cabriolet except that the rear section of roof opened, and price was somewhat higher at $7,190.

Style No. 1904 Sedan-Limousine. Some roofs were leather-covered, but this one has light-coloured English Burbank fabric. LeBaron felt the light upper body made the car look lower.

Interior view of Style No. 1904 Sedan-Limousine. The Cabriolet and Landaulet interiors were very similar

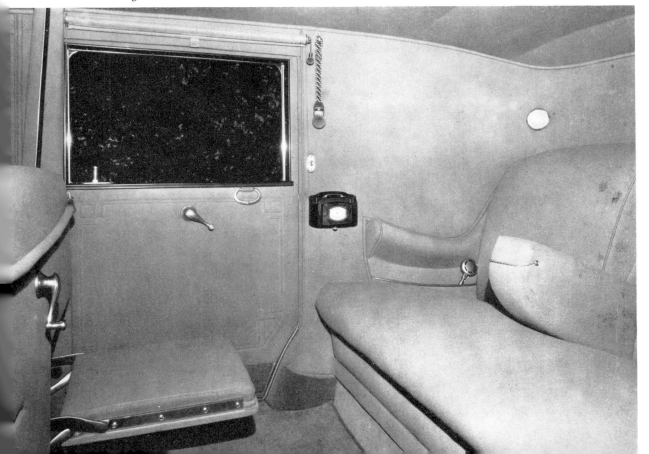

The companion Style No. 1905 had windows in the rear quarters and was slightly more expensive at $7,055.

Interior dimensions of Style No. 1905 Sedan-Limousine.

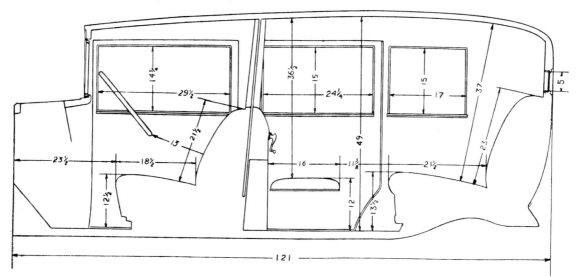

A larger model was Style No. 1907 All-weather Town Brougham, shown here in a rendering from LeBaron's catalogue. These renderings were usually painted by R. L. Stickney before the first car was built.

Actual photograph of Style No. 1907 shows how accurate the rendering was. This has chauffeur's canopy in place. Price was $7,055.

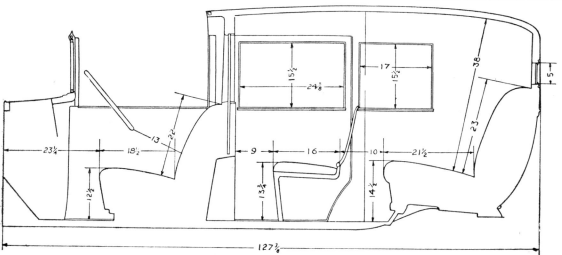

The same basic body was also available as Style No. 1909 Landaulet, with only a small section of the rear built to open. Price of this model was $7,440.

Interior dimensions of Style No. 1907 Brougham and Style No. 1909 Landaulet were identical.

This Sport Cabriolet was built specially for display during the 1930 New York Auto Show, but several duplicates were made. Ordered individually rather than in series, they sold for $9,275.

Two different renderings of the Convertible Roadster designed by the author for LeBaron early in 1930, on Model 745-C, showing the top up and also folded into its recess within the body.

One of the surviving LeBaron Convertible Roadsters, owned by Mr. Eugene Perkins of Indianapolis, Indiana, when this picture was taken. Fifty of these bodies were built and this is a late one on a Model 845 chassis.

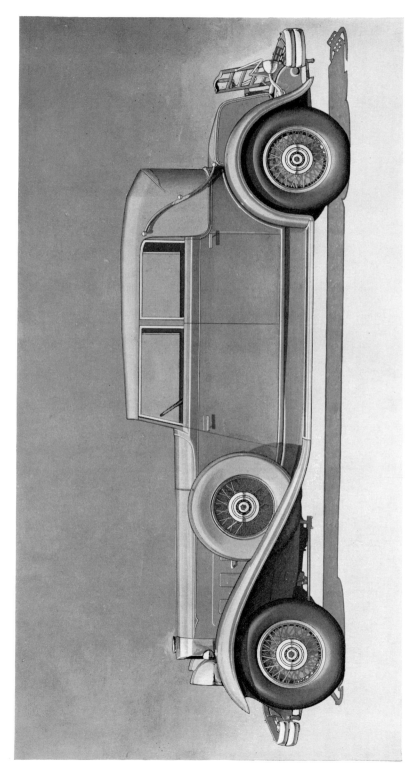

The original rendering by R. L. Stickney of LeBaron for this Convertible Sedan was done in 1930 and showed it on a Model 745-C. It was later modified to show a slight Vee in the radiator.

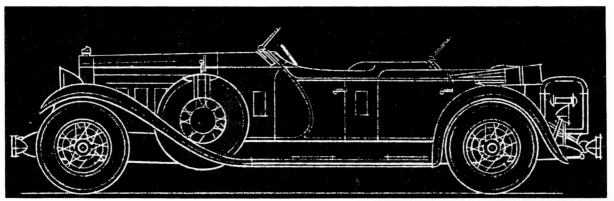

A dual-cowl Phaeton by LeBaron was sketched by Laurence Fellows for the magazine Vanity Fair.

One of the LeBaron Convertible Sedans of which a small series were built in 1930/31 with an overhead view of the interior, showing the elaborately tufted individual bucket seats.

This Sport Coupé built for the 1934 New York Auto Show was designed principally by Edward Macaulay of Packard. Although it has a Packard Custom Body Division plate, it was actually built by LeBaron.

A recent picture of the Model 1106 Sport Coupé, now owned by Mr. John G. Linhardt of Jamaica, New York.

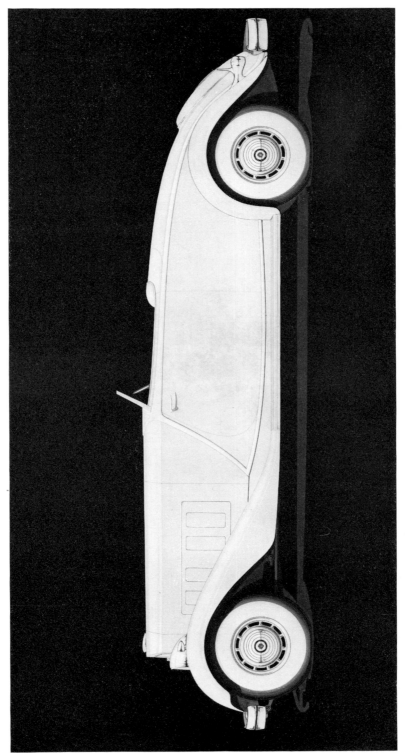

A rendering of one of the LeBaron designs that evolved into their Runabout on special short wheelbase Twelve for 1934.

A side-view of Style No. 275 Runabout, which sold for $7,745.

Rear view of the same Runabout shows the decided boat-tail.

Photographed during a special sports car display at the Henry Ford Museum, this LeBaron Runabout had some modifications worked bout by W. Everett Miller of Packard, and executed by Bohmann & Schwartz. It was ordered by Carole Lombard as a gift for Clark Gable, and is now in Gene Zimmerman's Autorama at Harrisburg, Pa.

A recent photograph of one LeBaron runabout, owned by Mr. Mark Sternheimer of Richmond, Virginia, who believes this car was first purchased by Douglas Fairbanks.

On Model 1108 Twelve, LeBaron built several of these Style No. 858 Town Cabriolets, which sold for $6,620 in 1934.

Somewhat larger was this Town Brougham on a 1936 Model 1408 Twelve. By this time, portions of the production body panels were being used in custom models. The car is owned by Mr. Louis Gravel of Montreal, Canada.

A Packard advertisement picturing Style L-395 Town Brougham. Like Mr. Gravel's car it sold for $6,435.

By 1937, LeBaron also had a Town Cabriolet on the shorter, 139-inch wheelbase Model 1507. Style L-394 sold for $5,700.

They built a series of these Sport Broughams, Style No. 1452, on the 1941 Model 180, which sold for $3,545, quite inexpensive for a custom body.

Another LeBaron model for 1941, on the long 148-inch wheelbase, this Limousine differed from the standard bodies and was more expensive at $5,595.

Interior of the Limousine was much more luxurious than the production models.

CHAPTER ELEVEN

Rollston

Founded in 1920 by Harry Loenschein and some associates, this coach-building firm on the west side of New York City was closely identified with Packard throughout its career, although they also built bodies on other chassis. Their early styling tended to be conservative, but the quality of the workmanship and finish of their bodies gained the approval of Grover Parvis at Packard's New York branch.

He ordered some small series of town cars from them, and also called on Rollston for special individual bodies for his most particular customers. Roadsters and phaetons came from the plant as well, and in the early 'thirties they built some attractive convertibles, but a good proportion of their bodies were formal town cars.

When Holbrook closed their doors in 1930, Rollston acquired some of their equipment and took on a good portion of their staff.

By 1937, some formal Panel Broughams on the smaller Model 120 chassis were ordered by Packard in an effort to stem the decline in demand for such vehicles by offering them at a lower price. A few were sold, but the day of the coachbuilt town car seemed over, and Mr. Loenschein decided to liquidate the company.

Rudy Creteur, who had done the designing and engineering and by now managed the shop, was more sanguine and purchased the bulk of the company's assets at auction. He set up a new firm of similar name, The Rollson Company, and over the next few years turned out some more elegant Packard town cars. The war put a stop to this, but Rollson stayed in business making galley equipment for submarines. A new plant in Plainview, Long Island, was built to handle the expanding volume and remains in business making similar items and yacht and steamship windows, but, alas, no coachbuilt bodies.

Rollston built this Town Cabriolet on Model 243 Eight for Mrs. W. E. Kimball of New York City. There were subtle design differences in some of their town cars, this one having a dropped rear quarter.

At the New York Auto Show in January, 1926, Packard's display included this Rollston Town Cabriolet, again subtly different from earlier ones especially in the treatment of rear door window mouldings.

Rollston did not build only town cars. This seven-passenger Phaeton on Model 243 Eight of 1925 had top irons made of corrosion-proof Monel Metal.

The rear of this Town Brougham on Model 243, photographed at the New York Salon of 1925. The horseshoe moulding on the rear panel was a favourite of Rollston's.

A year later, styles had changed and Packard had a Rollston All-weather Cabriolet on their New York Auto Show stand, with windows in the front doors in place of side-curtains. It is on Model 343.

At the New York Salon that Autumn, Rollston showed another All-weather Cabriolet on Model 443. The vertical Vee-windscreen was used on many of their town cars of the next few years.

Another All-weather Cabriolet on Model 443, again similar to the previous picture but with some small differences. This shows chauffeur's canopy in place.

Still another Model 443 Cabriolet has yet a different arrangement of mouldings and a polished aluminium panel running from radiator through the scuttle.

Rollston called this town car an "All-weather Quarter Window Cabriolet" when it was shown at the 1928 New York Salon. On Model 645, it was similar to their Town Broughams but with leather roof and decorative landau irons.

For Model 745-C, Rollston built some similar bodies but with metal roof edges, which they called Town Broughams, but the Packard catalogue listed them as Town Cars.

Rollston also built some Town Cabriolets on Model 745-C with slightly smaller body and closed rear quarters.
Interior dimensions of Rollston's Style No. 7509 All-weather Cabriolet, which sold for $10,085.

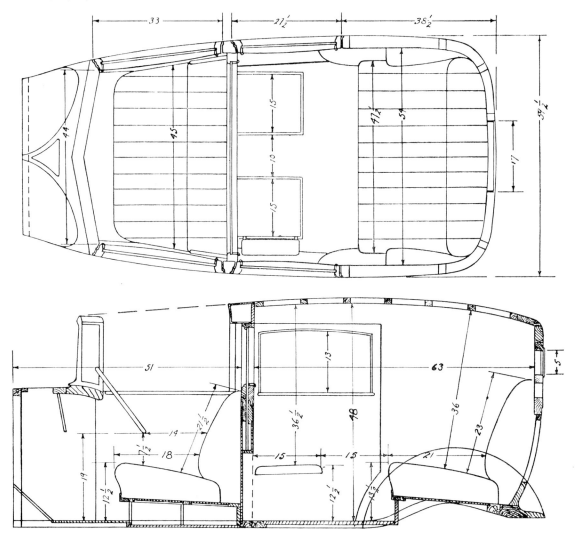

During 1928 and 1929, Rollston built some dashing Roadsters on Model 645, such as this one owned by Mr. Shelley D. Vincent of Mendon, Massachusetts.

Touring Cars were no longer being offered as standard models, so Rollston built a few such as this one on a Model 1502 Super Eight of 1937. It is owned by Mr. William C. Lund, Jr., of Minneapolis, Minnesota.

By 1936, demand for $10,000 town cars had dropped sharply. Rollston designed this Town Car for the smaller Model 120. At $3,975 it was the lowest priced Packard Town Car offered at that time.

Continuing the trend for Town Cars on the smaller Model 120, Rollston built this exquisite Panel Brougham in 1938. It is owned by the Pettit Collection of Louisa, Virginia.

They devised an ingenious improvement in the chauffeur's canopy on their later Town Cars. After the side panels were in place, a centre panel pulled out from under the rear roof, much in the manner of sedan sunroofs.

Not all Rollston Town Cars were on the small chassis. This Cabriolet was available on the Super Eight or Twelve of 1938, one of the last Rollston models.

Similar to the previous picture, this Town Cabriolet on Model 1708 Twelve carries the new name of Rollson. It is owned by Mr. George R. Augustson of Kansas City, Kansas.

This Panel Brougham, built in 1940 on Model 1801 Eight, found its way to France after the War and is now displayed at the Autorama Museum near Paris.

With rounded lines more like Rollson's Cabriolets, but with metal panelled roof sections, this was probably a special order.

From Packard's 1941 catalogue comes this view of a Rollson All-weather Cabriolet on the 138-inch wheelbase Model 180, priced at $4,695.

Interior of the Cabriolet was simple but luxurious. Note the side-facing auxiliary seat.

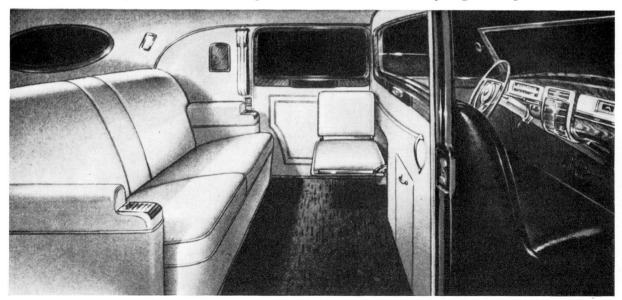

Somewhat larger was Rollson's All-weather Town Car on the 148-inch wheelbase chassis from the same catalogue. It sold for $4,820.

Interior of the Town Car was similar in effect to the Cabriolet, but added space allowed for forward-facing auxiliary seats.

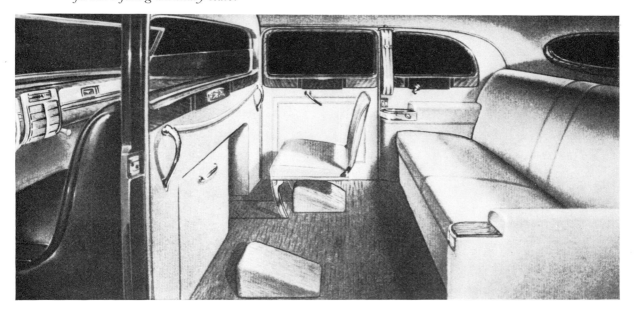

Rollston continued to build a few of the Panel Broughams designed for Model 120, but mounted on the 127-inch wheelbase Model 1906 used for the Darrin Convertibles. This one is owned by Dr. Larry Quirk of Tucson, Arizona.

CHAPTER TWELVE

Waterhouse

Although short-lived as coachbuilders go, this company made quite an impact during the few years of its existence.

Charles L. and M. Sargent Waterhouse had each spent some years with Judkins and were hardly tyros. In fact, their father had earlier been a key Judkins employee. In 1928, they obtained some financial backing and opened their own factory in Webster, Massachusetts. The original announcement said it was "to build bodies for duPont cars," and they did produce some for that make.

The following year, Packard's export department was searching for someone to produce a car for exhibition at the Paris Salon, along the lines of a drophead coupé which Van den Plas had done for them a year earlier. I am not certain why this search began so late, but Waterhouse was the only coachbuilder willing to undertake the task and promise to have the car completed in the period of less than two months which was available.

Even before it was shipped to the Paris Salon, the car caught the eye of Alvan Macaulay, Packard's President, when he visited the New York branch just as the car was being prepared for shipment. Orders for a series of duplicates followed, as well as for some other designs.

Unfortunately, by this time the stock market crash had had a severe impact on the coachbuilding industry, and the still fledgling concern could not long survive. Their doors closed in 1933, just a few years after they had opened.

A view of the Waterhouse Convertible with top folded. The car was low, but contrasting lower body panels make it seem even lower.

A restored Waterhouse Victoria. The side-mounted spares and different colour scheme somewhat change its appearance.

Not all Waterhouse Packards were Convertible Victorias. They also built one or two Sedans such as this.

The Packard stand at the 1931 New York Auto Show, with the rear of a redesigned Waterhouse Convertible Victoria at far left. The folding top had been modified to fit into a recess in the body.

A recently discovered rendering of a Waterhouse design for a later model. It appears to date from early 1933, just before Waterhouse went out of business, and was never actually built.

Another rendering of the new Waterhouse design, which also had the top folding partly into the body.

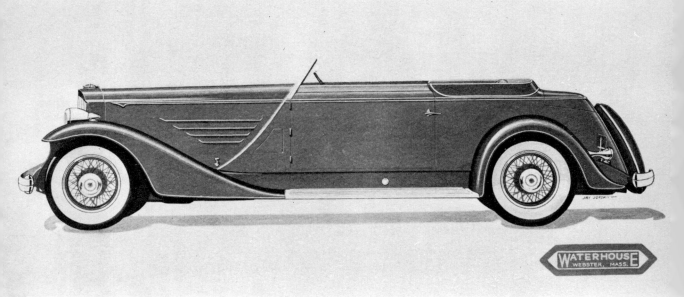

CHAPTER THIRTEEN

Willoughby

The Willoughby family had been in the carriage business in Rome, New York, before the advent of the automobile, but set up a factory in nearby Utica as their business grew and they began making bodies for cars. Some of their early work was in small production runs for relatively high-priced cars, but they also turned out truly custom bodies even then, and by the mid-twenties this was their sole business.

The company's greatest success came under the direction of Francis D. Willoughby, who had succeeded his father as head of the company on the latter's sudden death in 1908. Still a young man, Francis Willoughby had already served an apprentice period with several competitors. This was a not unusual practice at the time.

Willoughby were especially noted for the fine quality of their upholstery, whereas their styling was usually quite conservative. This brought them orders for some small series of Packard limousines during the mid-twenties, as well as an occasional town car.

They had also attracted the eye of Edsel Ford and his orders for Lincoln kept them going during the depression years until they finally closed down in 1938.

Interior of a Willoughby Packard Coupé of 1925. Note beamed ceiling effect with varnished wood framing deliberately left exposed.

A seven-passenger Limousine on 1926 Model 243 Eight.

Although Willoughby's Limousines were conservative, their Town Cars were often less so. The cetnre car built in 1926 on Model 243 had traditional coachlamps and an unusual moulding treatment.

This seven-passenger Sedan is subtly different from the Limousine pictured earlier, although also built in 1926.

A Sedan from late 1926 has more rounded lines and an integral sun visor.

A more compact Sedan-Limousine built in late 1928 on Model 645. Willoughby showed such a car at the New York Salon that year.

CHAPTER FOURTEEN

Other American Coachbuilders

There were many more American coachbuilders in the early part of the century, some of whom did not survive the rigorous competition of the 1920s when styling became an important concept. Some others grew too large to bother with handcrafted bodies, went into other fields, or were absorbed in the various mergers of that time.

The work of some of these is illustrated herein, and a list follows with some brief comments:

Bohman & Schwartz, Pasadena, California. Set up by former employees of the Walter M. Murphy Company as a successor to that firm.

Brunn & Company, Buffalo, N.Y. One of America's best custom body builders, closely identified for some years with Lincoln, but who built some attractive Packards late in their career.

Demarest & Company, New York, N.Y., and earlier in New Haven, Connecticut, as A. T. Demarest & Co.

Farnham & Nelson, Roslindale, Mass.

Hayes Body Company, Grand Rapids, Mich. Primarily a production body firm, who built some experimental bodies while Alexis de Sakhnoffsky was their designer.

John S. Inskip, Inc. See remarks under Brewster & Co.

Limousine Body Co., Kalamazoo, Mich. Primarily builders of low-volume production models.

Locke & Company, New York City and Rochester, N.Y. One of America's finest coachbuilders, later building small series of bodies.

Walter M. Murphy & Company, Pasadena, California. Built many special bodies for Hollywood personalities.

Phillips Custom Body Company, Warren, Ohio. Earlier the Phillips Carriage Company. Best known for convertible coupes in the mid-twenties.

Leon Rubay & Company, Cleveland, Ohio. A leading coachbuilder of the early part of the century, who unfortunately tried unsuccessfully, to make a complete car of their own, in 1922.

W. S. Seaman Company, Milwaukee, Wisc. Builders of custom and production bodies who became closely associated with Nash and absorbed by that company, one of the predecessors of the American Motors Corp.

A special Convertible Coupé on 1910 Model 30. The coachbuilder is not identified in Packard's files, but it is obviously a special body with extensive canework decoration.

Packard's files call this *1909 Model 18* Landaulet a "Taxi" and it may have been built for
that purpose. Again the coachbuilder was not identified.
Another special body, this Phaeton on *1910 Model 30* is also unidentified. There seem to be
slip covers made of the top material, presumably to protect the leather upholstery in event
of a sudden shower.

Packard's files identify this only as a "Special Limousine" on Single Six of 1922, one of the few coachbuilt bodies on that chassis.

An armoured Limousine built for Manchurian war lord Tsan Tso Lin on a 1921/2 Twin Six. No body builder's plate is visible, but it looks like some Holbrook or Fleetwood bodies of the period.

Bohman & Schwartz built this Convertible Sedan in 1941 on Model 180. Lines are lower than standard bodies of the time, and both doors hinge at centre.

Another Bohman & Schwartz body from the same year, this Enclosed Drive Limousine also differs from production models, with doors again hung from the centre, as on many earlier Murphy bodies.

Brunn built several such Limousines for the 1939 Model 1708 Twelve. This one is owned by Mr. George Tilp of Short Hills, New Jersey. The coloured glass inserts above the windscreen were a Brunn innovation. This model sold for $8,355.

Brunn also made some Town Cars of partly similar design. This one on a 1938 Model 1608 Twelve belongs to ex-racer Phil Hill of Santa Monica, California.

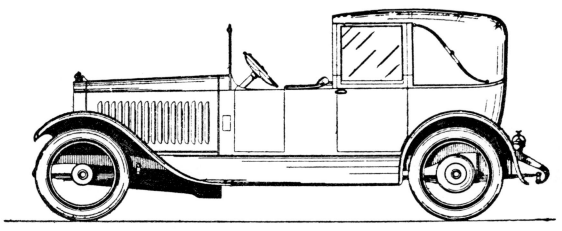

At the 1921 New York Salon, Demarest & Company showed this Cabriolet on a Twin-six.

A Demarest Cabriolet similar to the one they showed at the Salon.

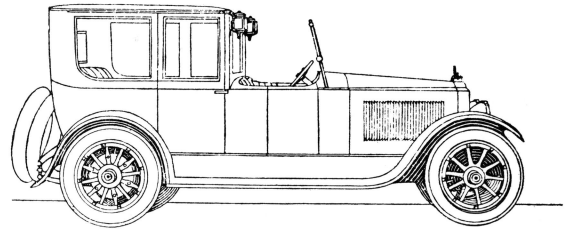

Another Packard at that 1921 Salon was this Limousine-Brougham by Farnham & Nelson.

In the chapter on Judkins is the first Touring Sedan built by that company with removable posts. By 1922, Packard ordered a series of similar bodies from the Limousine Body Company for the Single Six.

While planning their revived Twin-six, Packard built an experimental front-wheel drive chassis, fitted with a special body by Hayes to disguise it. Alexis de Sakhnoffsky, who had left Van den Plas to become Hayes' chief designer, conceived it.

Locke & Company built this Phaeton of special design on a 1926 Model 343 Eight.

Another Locke body on Model 343 was this Sedan-Limousine with closed rear quarters.

Walter M. Murphy Company showed this "Clear Vision Sedan" at the 1927 New York Salon. Although it had a fixed roof, the framed windows and narrow posts were like those on their Convertible Sedans.

Murphy built many open cars for the mild Californian climate, such as this Model 443 Phaeton of 1928.

Another Murphy body on Model 443, this Roadster was one of their early designs with semi-disappearing top.

The Phillips Custom Body Company specialized in Convertible Coupés, often built in series. This one on a Model 243 was an individual design.

The chassis is Packard but the body is by Pierce-Arrow. Mrs. John D. Gordon of Norwalk, Connecticut, purchased a Pierce-Arrow Limousine in 1917. She did not like the styling of newer cars and had the body remounted first on a later Pierce-Arrow, and then in 1937 on a Model 1508 Packard Twelve. The car is now owned by the Museum of Automobiles at Petit Jean Mountain, Arkansas, founded by the late Governor Winthrop Rockefeller.

An undated Rubay catalogue of about 1917 includes the three above illustrations.
Top, the Diana Roadster on a Twin-six chassis.
Centre, a seven-passenger Touring Car called the "Botha".
Bottom, an Enclosed-drive Limousine called a "Colonial Convertible Berline".

A 1916 Twin-six Sedan by W. S. Seaman Company, a firm which later merged into Nash and is a predecessor of American Motors Corporation, who supplied these photographs.

Another Seaman Sedan, somewhat sleeker and probably built later. Both Seaman sedans have only a single door in the centre of each side.

This Seaman Roadster on a 1917 Twin-six, also from the American Motors archives, was quite similar to the production models.

Much smoother lines indicate this Seaman Phaeton was probably built later in 1917.

Another Seaman Roadster, this larger four-passenger model is of the type called a "Chummy Roadster" in 1917 when it was built.

CHAPTER FIFTEEN

European Coachbuilders

Since Packard maintained a very active export department, many of their chassis were shipped abroad to be fitted with coachwork from local firms to suit the taste of those countries. The English coachbuilders represented include some of the finest —

Barker & Company
Carlton Carriage Company
Freestone & Webb
Hooper & Company
H. J. Mulliner & Company
Salmons & Sons

On the Continent, a similarly choice group of firms are represented among the photographs herein —

Baxter-Gallé of France
Henri Chapron of France
Franay of France
Gläser of Germany
Graber of Switzerland
Hibbard & Darrin of France
Hofslageribolaget of Sweden
Kellner & Cie of France
Neusse of Germany
Gustav Nordbergs of Sweden
Norrmalms of Sweden
Van den Plas of Belgium

Barker built this fully-collapsible Sedan-Limousine on a 1922 Model 133 Six. This design was much admired in the United States, and several American coachbuilders adopted some of its features.

Barker & Company built this Sedan-Landaulette on a 1929 Model 645 Super Eight, with folding rear roof section. Styling is quite conservative.

By 1938, Barker's designs were more dashing, as in this Sedanca de Ville on a Super Eight.

Baxter-Gallé of Paris did this rendering of a Roadster on Model 645 Eight of 1939, but it is not known whether it was ever built.

Much the same date as the Barker on the opposite page is this Sedanca de Ville by Carlton Carriage Co.

Henri Chapron built some elegant bodies on the smaller Packards. This 1937 Drop-head Coupé or Convertible Victoria on Model 120-C, owned by Mr. Paul Womersley of Bradford, Yorkshire, may be the only survivor.

Another French firm, Franay, built this Town Car on a 1937 Super Eight, shown here at an auto show.

Another Franay body, this one a Limousine on a 1939 Model 1706 Super Eight.

Rear view of the 1939 Franay Limousine shows the razor-edge styling.

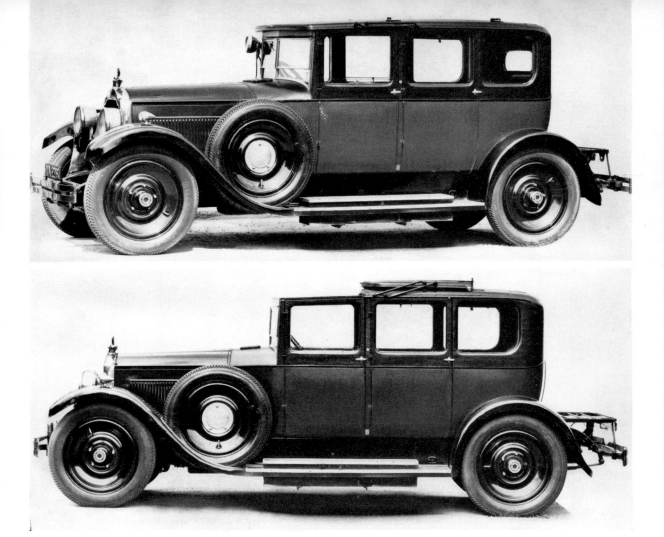

Freestone & Webb supplied this Sunroof Saloon on a 1925 Model 333 Six. Lower view shows the roof section over the front seat folded back. The lines are typical of British coachwork of the period.

This Freestone & Webb fully-collapsible Sedan on a somewhat later Model 433 Six, has sleeker lines.

While the previous Freestone & Webb bodies were on the six-cylinder chassis, this one is on an Eight, probably Model 336 of 1926/7.

By 1938, Freestone & Webb's coachwork was becoming more streamlined, even such large bodies as this Limousine on an Eight, chassis no. 502281.

A Convertible Sedan by Glaser of Dresden, Germany, on a 1933 Model 1002 Eight.

The Glaser Convertible Sedan with roof folded. Germans preferred well-padded roofs which looked well closed, but were quite bulky when folded.

Graber in Switzerland built many Packards, especially Drop-head Coupés (or Convertible Victorias) such as this one on a 1931 Model 833, now owned by a German, Mr. Lutz.

Another Graber Convertible Victoria, this on 1932 Model 901, is owned by Mr. George L. Verhoeven of Boom, Belgium.

Hibbard & Darrin built this Convertible Victoria on a 1929 Model 645 chassis. It has their typical rolled-belt treatment through the doors. The interior was photographed at the Packard factory after being shipped from France.

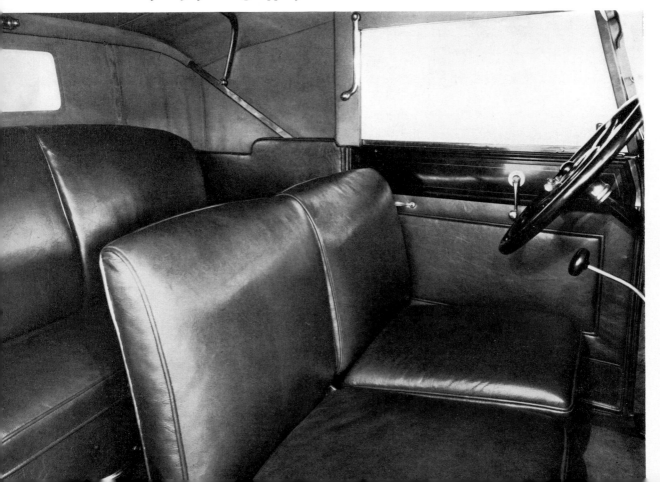

Singer Al Jolson with his 1928 Model 443 Convertible Sedan by Hibbard & Darrin, disguised with a radiator much like a Hispano-Suiza.

This Hibbard & Darrin Town Car on Model 745 was planned for the 1929 New York Salon. Special mudguards somewhat disguise it.

Hooper & Company built this Landaulette de Ville on a 1925 Model 333 Six. The smaller chassis was popular in Britain for such formal bodies.

A later Hooper body of more graceful shape, this Limousine is on a 1935/6 Model 1203 Eight.

From H. J. Mulliner in England came this Sedan on a Model 443 Eight of 1928, the lower view showing the ingenious concealed luggage compartment. Bodies of this style were mounted on Rolls-Royce Phantom Ones and Speed Six Bentleys.

A Kellner Town Cabriolet on Model 243 chassis of 1925/6.

Kellner of Paris built such Sedanca de Villes in the thirties on various chassis, deliberately designed to look like a Dual-cowl Phaeton. This one on a Model 1608 Twelve of 1938 belongs to Harrah's Automobile Collection of Reno, Nevada.

Profile view of Harrah's Kellner Packard, showing the rear superstructure in more detail.

A sporting two-seater on a Twin-six from Sweden, built by Hofslageribolaget of Stockholm on a 1919 chassis that seems to have been shortened. Note the boat-tail and special mudguards. Neusse in Germany built this Convertible Coupé — called a "Cabriolet" in Germany — on what may be a Model 633 chassis. The special equipment with which it was fitted make identification difficult.

An unusual body from Gustav Nordbergs of Stockholm, this Limousine on a 1925 Model 243 Eight was panelled in mahogany.

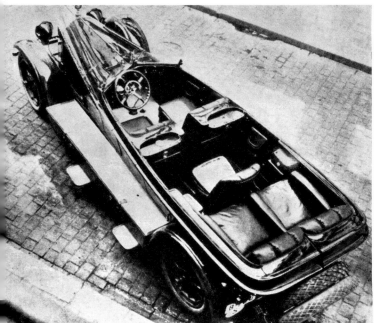

Two views of a special Tourer by Gustav Nordbergs on a late Twin-six, lengthened and disguised. Interior view shows the unusual seating arrangement. It was built for publisher Eric Akerlund.

More formal is this Town Brougham, also by Gustav Nordbergs, on Model 243 Eight.

Norrmalms of Stockholm built this Convertible Sedan on Model 443 of 1928. Note unusual sloping edge of rear windows.

The Norrmalms Convertible Sedan with roof folded.

Somewhat Germanic in styling is this Cabriolet, or Convertible Victoria, also by Norrmalms on a 1938 Model 120.

Salmons in England were well known for their "Tickford" Drop-head Coupés on many medium-priced chassis. This one is on a 1938 Model 120.

Van den Plas in Belgium built this "Faux Cabriolet" or non-collapsible Town Car on a 1926 Model 343. It won a prize at the Monte Carlo Concours d'Elegance.

Another Van den Plas body on a Model 443 was very low for its time, only 66 inches to the top of the roof.

The young lady driving this Twin-six Phaeton seems to have moved her chauffeur to the rear seat. The car was photographed and possibly modified in England.

This Tourer on a 1923 six-cylinder chassis is definitely British in details, but its coachbuilder is not identified.

A German coachbuilder, also unidentified, produced this "Cabriolet" on a 1928 Model 443. Some of the lines resemble Erdmann & Rossi bodies.

Finally, the builder of this French Sedan on a 1938 Eight is also unknown. The sweeping lines could have come from any of several French coachbuilders.

BREWSTER & CO
NEW YORK

Dietrich Inc.
DETROIT.

FLEETWOOD

HOLBROOK
HUDSON, N.Y.

JUDKINS

LeBaron

WILLOUGHBY